COMMITTEE ON
POPULATION AND DEMOGRAPHY Report No. 27

Rapid Population Change in China, 1952-1982

Ansley J. Coale
Committee on Population and
  Demography
Commission on Behavioral and
  Social Sciences and Education
National Research Council

NATIONAL ACADEMY PRESS
Washington, D.C.   1984

NOTICE: The project that is the subject of this report was approved by the Governing Board of the National Research Council, whose members are drawn from the councils of the National Academy of Sciences, the National Academy of Engineering, and the Institute of Medicine. The members of the committee responsible for the report were chosen for their special competences and with regard for appropriate balance.

This report has been reviewed by a group other than the authors according to procedures approved by a Report Review Committee consisting of members of the National Academy of Sciences, the National Academy of Engineering, and the Institute of Medicine.

The National Research Council was established by the National Academy of Sciences in 1916 to associate the broad community of science and technology with the Academy's purposes of furthering knowledge and of advising the federal government. The Council operates in accordance with general policies determined by the Academy under the authority of its congressional charter of 1863, which establishes the Academy as a private, nonprofit, self-governing membership corporation. The Council has become the principal operating agency of both the National Academy of Sciences and the National Academy of Engineering in the conduct of their services to the government, the public, and the scientific and engineering communities. It is administered jointly by both Academies and the Institute of Medicine. The National Academy of Engineering and the Institute of Medicine were established in 1964 and 1970, respectively, under the charter of the National Academy of Sciences.

Library of Congress Catalog Card Number 84-61188

International Standard Book Number 0-309-03480-9

Available from

NATIONAL ACADEMY PRESS
2101 Constitution Avenue, N.W.
Washington, D.C. 20418

Printed in the United States of America

COMMITTEE ON POPULATION AND DEMOGRAPHY

ANSLEY J. COALE (Chair), Office of Population Research
    Princeton University
WILLIAM BRASS, Centre for Population Studies, London
    School of Hygiene and Tropical Medicine
LEE-JAY CHO, East-West Population Institute, East-West
    Center, Honolulu
RONALD FREEDMAN, Population Studies Center, University
    of Michigan
NATHAN KEYFITZ, Department of Sociology, Harvard
    University
LESLIE KISH, Institute for Social Research, University
    of Michigan
W. PARKER MAULDIN, Population Division, The Rockefeller
    Foundation
JANE MENKEN, Office of Population Research, Princeton
    University
SAMUEL PRESTON, Population Studies Center, University of
    Pennsylvania
WILLIAM SELTZER, Statistical Office, United Nations
CONRAD TAEUBER, Kennedy Institute, Center for Population
    Research, Georgetown University
ETIENNE VAN DE WALLE, Population Studies Center,
    University of Pennsylvania

ROBERT J. LAPHAM, Study Director

Note: Members of the Committee and its panel and working groups participated in this project in their individual capacities; the listing of their organizational affiliation is for identification purposes only, and the views and designations used in this report are not necessarily those of the organizations mentioned.

CONTENTS

LIST OF TABLES   vii

LIST OF FIGURES   ix

PREFACE   xi

SUMMARY   1

1   INTRODUCTION   8

    Scope of the Report, 8
    Background, 9

2   SOURCES AND QUALITY OF DATA   12

    Data Sources, 12

        Census and Fertility Survey Data, 12
        Independence of the Data Sources, 13
        Characteristics of the 1982 Census and
            Fertility Survey, 15

    Quality of Data, 18

        Data by Single Years of Age, 18
        Abnormal Ratios of Men to Women in Census and
            Survey Data, 21
        Official Data on Births and Deaths, 27
        Data on Children and Marriage, 31
        Quality of Data: Summary, 37

3 MARRIAGE IN CHINA SINCE 1950   39

    Proportion Ever-Married Women and the
       First-Marriage Rate, 39
    Mean Age at First Marriage, 41
    Patterns of Marriage, 42

4 CHILDBEARING IN CHINA SINCE 1950   46

    Total Fertility Rates, 46
    The Effect of Changes in Nuptiality on the
       Rate of Childbearing, 48
    Age Patterns of Marital Fertility, 54
    Differential Fertility, 58

        Urban/Rural Differences, 58
        Han and Minority Group Differences, 62
        Other Fertility Determinants, 62

    Contraceptive Practice in China, 62

5 MORTALITY IN CHINA   64

    Methods, 64
    Life Tables, 66
    Crude Death Rates, 66
    Variation Over Time, 70

6 CONCLUSIONS   71

   NOTES   73

    APPENDIX: DATA TABLES   75

   REFERENCES   87

LIST OF TABLES

1. Annual Number of Births (in millions) from Official Figures and as Calculated from Fertility Rates in Survey and Interpolated Populations, and Estimated Completenes of Reporting, 1953-82 28
2. Total Number of Children Ever Born to Women Classified in Five-Year Age Intervals, 1982 33
3. Estimated Fiscal Year Births, 1951-52 to 1981-82, Number Recorded in Corresponding Cohort in 1982, and Proportion Surviving 35
4. Proportion of Children Surviving Among Children Ever Born Alive to Women Aged 15-19 to 50-54, 1982 36
5. Birth Rate and Total Fertility Rate Derived from Fertility Survey 47
6. Total Fertility Rate Calculated for Selected Years, from Proportion of Women Ever Married and Age-Specific Marital Fertility Rates, 1956 51
7. Annual Births (in millions), Total Fertility Rate, 1970-82 53
8. Total Fertility Rates, Rural and Urban Populations, 1950-81 59
9. Abridged Life Tables, Male and Female, 1953-64 and 1964-82 67
10. Crude Death Rates (per 1,000), 1953-81 69

A-1. Calculated Number of Women by Single Years of Age, Aged 15-49 for Each Year, Estimated by Cohort Interpolation (in 100s), 1953-82 76
A-2. Population by Sex and Single Years of Age, 1953, 1964, and 1982 (after adjustment) 78

A-3	Proportion of Children Born Alive Who Were Born in Specified Years, by Age of Mother, 1982	81
A-4	Proportion of Ever-Married Women (per 1,000 women) by Single Years of Age, Aged 15-35, Constructed from First Marriage Rates, 1950-81, and Reported in the Sample Survey, 1982	82
A-5	Number of Ever-Married Women (in 100s) by Duration Since First Marriage, 1970-82	84
A-6	Number of Births and Marital Fertility Rate at Each Duration of Marriage, 1970, 1977, and 1981	85

LIST OF FIGURES

1	Total Fertility Rates for Urban and Rural Areas and for China, 1952-82	5
2	Age Pyramid of the Population, 1982	6
3	Death Rates (per 1,000) from Recorded Deaths and Adjusted for Underreporting, 1953-82	7
4	Proportion of Females Surviving Between Successive Censuses for Each Age	19
5	Number of Persons Under Age 30 in 1982 and Number of Persons Under Age 11 in 1964 (in millions) by Single Years of Age, as Projected and Enumerated in the Census	22
6	Sex Ratio (males per 100 females) by Single Years of Age, 1953, 1964, and 1982	23
7	Sex Ratio (males per 100 females) by Year of Birth for Censuses of 1953, 1964, and 1982	24
8	Completeness of Recording of Births, 1953-81	29
9	Total Female First-Marriage Rate (sum of first marriage frequencies), 1950-82	40
10	Mean Age at First Marriage of Females, 1950-82	42
11	Proportion of Ever-Married Women, by Single Years of Age, Cohorts Aged 15 in 1950, 1960, 1965, 1970, and 1973	43
12	Proportion of Ever-Married Women, Cohorts Aged 15 in 1950, 1960, 1965, 1970, and 1973 and Standard Curves Fitted to Ages 16.5 and 20.5	44
13	Ratio of Age-Specific Marital Fertility to Natural Fertility, 1956, 1961, 1970, 1975, and 1980	56
14	Total Fertility Rates, Rural and Urban Populations, 1950-81	60
15	Age-Specific Fertility Rates, Rural and Urban Populations, 1955, 1968, and 1980	61
16	Age-Specific Fertility Rates, Ethnic Minority Women and Rural Han Women, 1981	63
17	Age-Specific Mortality Rates, Females, 1953-64, 1964-82, 1973-75, and 1978	68

PREFACE

This report, using analyses of recently available census and survey data on the population of China, presents the demographic history of China during the past 30 years. The report uses detailed assessments of data from a major 1982 fertility survey and the 1982 census of China, which became available at the end of 1983, to develop estimates of three major population processes for 1952-82: fertility, nuptiality, and mortality.

With the rapid expansion in world population in recent decades, fertility and its determinants have been urgent topics for research. Attempts to affect population growth have focused on reducing fertility, with some apparent effect. The peak rate of growth in the world's population has now passed although growth is still at a high level in almost all the developing countries. In absolute numbers, the increase in the world's population continues to rise: according to United Nations medium projections, more people will be added each year for the next 35-40 years than were added in 1980. In this context, China's recent rapid declines in fertility and mortality are remarkable; moreover, China's decline in fertility has contributed substantially to the modest reduction in the world rate of population growth.

This report on China is number 27 in a series of reports prepared by the Committee on Population and Demography and its several panels. (A complete list of these reports is printed on the inside back cover.) The committee was established in 1977 by the Commission on Behavioral and Social Sciences and Education of the National Research Council (NRC). Funded for a period of 5-1/2 years by the Agency for International Development (AID), the committee undertook three major tasks:

1. To evaluate available evidence and prepare estimates of levels and trends of fertility and mortality in selected developing nations;

2. To improve the technologies for estimating fertility and mortality when only incomplete or inadequate data exist (including techniques of data collection); and

3. To evaluate the factors determining the changes in birth rates in less developed nations.

About half of the reports resulting from these tasks are concerned with demographic estimates in less-developed countries and with methodology and the other half are concerned with the determinants of fertility.

In its early deliberations about which countries to include in its work, the committee did not select China for several reasons, primarily the nonavailability of an adequate data base for a scientific assessment of fertility and mortality trends. At that time, it was not foreseen that it would be possible later on to prepare a comprehensive report on the demography of China. However, the committee was interested in China, and, with cosponsorship by the NRC's Committee on Scholarly Communication with the People's Republic of China and modest support from the U.S. Department of State, a workshop on population research in China was held at the National Academy of Sciences in October 1980; the proceedings were published by the National Academy Press in 1981.

This report on China has been made possible by a grant from The Rockefeller Foundation and with support from the NRC Fund.*

---

*The National Research Council (NRC) Fund is a pool of private, discretionary, non-federal funds that is used to support a program of Academy-initiated studies of national issues in which science and technology figure significantly. The NRC Fund consists of contributions from: a consortium of private foundations including the Carnegie Corporation of New York, the Charles E. Culpeper Foundation, the William and Flora Hewlett Foundation, the John D. and Catherine T. MacArthur Foundation, the Andrew W. Mellon Foundation, the Rockefeller Foundation, and the Alfred P. Sloan Foundation; the Academy Industry Program,

The committee and the National Research Council wish to thank Ansley J. Coale for preparing this report, and indeed for doing so within such a short period of time. Sincere thanks are also extended to the reviewers who both read the report on short notice and attended a review meeting in Washington in April 1984. Several other individuals assisted in the production of this report. Marleen Stern and Kathryn Reynolds typed the draft and tables in Princeton, and Barbara Vaughan assisted with computer tabulations. At the NRC, Lucy Santiago typed the camera-ready copy of text and tables, Eugenia Grohman edited the report, and Elaine McGarraugh handled all of the production editing details. The committee extends its gratitude to these individuals for their contributions to the report.

Finally, this is a fitting occasion to thank Ansley J. Coale for his leadership of the Committee on Population and Demography and his many contributions to its products. The committee's extensive accomplishments owe much to those contributions and especially to his effectiveness as committee chair.

Robert J. Lapham, Study Director
Committee on Population and Demography

---

which seeks annual contributions from companies that are concerned with the health of U.S. science and technology and with public policy issues with technological content; and the National Academy of Sciences and the National Academy of Engineering endowments.

SUMMARY

In 1982 the People's Republic of China carried out a census with a more comprehensive interview schedule than ever before employed in China and using a very large, carefully chosen, and extensively trained field staff. The census was preceded by pilot surveys to test the instruments and field procedures. A tabulation of 10 percent of the individual returns has been completed, published in China, and made available abroad in limited circulation. Also in 1982 a fertility survey covering a very large sample of households (total population of more than 1 million) was conducted in China, and its results have been published in great detail in a special issue of the Chinese Journal Population and Economics. In addition, the distribution of the population by sex and single years of age as enumerated in the censuses of 1953 and 1964 has been recently released. This new information, supplemented by time series of registered births and deaths and end-of-year population totals extending back to the 1950s and by data from other large recent surveys, provides a sound basis for constructing an accurate and detailed history of the remarkable changes in fertility, mortality, and marriage that have occurred in China since the People's Republic was established.

The newly available information includes complete histories of marriage and childbearing of women up to age 67 in the 1/1,000 fertility survey of 1982. The responses have been analyzed and tabulated in the form of marriage rates and birth rates by single years of age in single calendar years from 1950 to 1981. When the survey data are combined and compared with the census data for 1953, 1964, and 1982 on numbers of persons by sex and single years of age, they pass a series of stringent tests of accuracy and consistency. The same analysis reveals that official data on birth and death rates have understated the true numbers by a considerable margin. The tests support the substantive findings in this report on levels and changes in fertility, nuptiality, and mortality in China since 1950.

Fertility Rates. The birth rate in China has been higher than that listed in official sources. In the 1950s the birth rate was generally above 40 per 1,000 until a precipitous fall--from 42.5 per 1,000 in 1957 to 21.9 in 1961--that coincided with the Great Leap Forward and the ensuing years of economic disruption and famine. The post-crisis peak birth rate in 1963 was just short of 50 births per 1,000.

A more useful fertility measure, the total fertility rate (TFR)--the average number of children that would be born in a lifetime to women subject to the birth rates by age in a given period--was about 6.0 before the Great Leap Forward, declined to 3.3 in 1961, rose to 7.5 in 1963, returned to 6.0 in the mid-1960s, fell steeply to only 2.2 in 1980, and then rose slightly to over 2.6 in 1981 and 1982. The birth data on which these fertility rates are based are derived from the new detailed information, especially that from the fertility survey. It is clear that the number of births previously listed in official sources has been incomplete: by more than 15 percent in the 1950s, by less than 10 percent in the late 1960s and early 1970s, and by 15 percent or more since the intensification of the antinatalist program in 1979.

Age Pattern of Fertility. The age pattern of fertility of married women in the 1950s was a pattern of gradual decline in the rate of childbearing with age until age 30; the decline steepened after age 30 and especially after age 35. This age pattern closely resembles the early gradual and later steep decline of marital fertility rates with age of woman that is characteristic of populations in which couples practice little contraception or induced abortion. This age pattern of marital fertility in the 1950s supports the inference of little use of contraception. In the 1970s (and especially in 1980), by contrast, marital fertility rates fell very steeply with age of women after their late 20s, a pattern characteristic of very general resort to contraception to limit fertility after desired family size is reached.

In 1961, when the TFR fell to only a little more than half the TFR of 1955 or 1957, the fertility of married women was very much reduced at all ages. A nearly uniform reduction in fertility at different ages is consistent with a quasi-biological cause of low fertility--i.e., low fertility was the result of disruption of normal life and famine-induced subfecundity rather than a large increase in the use of contraception. The unmatched post-crisis TFR of 7.5 in 1963 involved peak marital fertility rates at all ages. These high rates at all ages may also have a quasi-biological explanation. Newly married couples (there was a very high first-marriage rate in 1962) and couples resuming normal life are especially susceptible to the risk of childbearing since few of the women are protected from the risk of pregnancy because of nursing a previously born child.

Contraceptive Use. In 1981 contraception--mostly sterilization, the IUD, and contraceptive pills--was practiced by more than two-thirds of married women aged 15 to 49.

Mean Age at First Marriage. The mean age at first marriage of women was about 18.5 years in the 1940s, about a year older than that estimated for rural China in 1930. The mean age at marriage rose gradually (with some fluctuations) to a little more than 20 in 1970, and then steeply to more than 23 in 1979. There was then a slight decline, of about four- tenths a year, to a mean age of 22.7 years in the first half of 1982.

Effects on Fertility of Changes in Mean Age at First Marriage. The changing age of entry into marriage contributed strongly to changes in fertility. Had the noncontraceptive marital fertility rates at each age of the 1950s continued, the increase in age at marriage by itself, by exempting many younger women from the risk of childbearing, would have led to a TFR in 1980 that was 20 percent below the TFR of 1950--a hypothetical decline about one-third as great as the actual one. The rise in age at marriage in the 1970s would have produced (by a different mechanism) a 20 percent reduction in the TFR during that decade even if from 1970 on married women had successfully attained unchanging goals of restricted family size. This apparently anomalous effect--a 20 percent decline in TFR even though married women produce an unchanging total number of children per marriage-- arises from the temporary reduction in the number of marriages that is caused by a rise in mean age at marriage. About one-third of the reduction in the TFR from 1970 to 1980 was associated with the increase in age at marriage and would have occurred with constant duration-specific marital fertility rates.

When mean age at marriage ceases to rise, the diminution in the number of marriages caused by rising age at marriage ceases, and the number of the newly married women increases. In 1980-82 a sharp increase in the total first-marriage rate accompanied the termination and slight reversal of the increase in mean age at marriage. Most of the upturn in TFR after 1980 was the result of the marriage boom in 1980-82 and would have occurred with constant fertility rates at each duration of marriage. Upward pressure on the TFR will continue because the highest marital fertility rates occur one or two years after the date of marriage; the large number of marriages in 1981 and 1982 will inflate births in 1983 and 1984 even if the recently married have only one or two children.

Urban/Rural and Other Fertility Differences. Before the temporary sharp decline in the TFR that began in 1958, the TFR in the cities was about 10 percent below the rural TFR; about half of the difference in fertility can be ascribed to later marriage in the urban population. As shown in Figure 1, between 1960 and 1966, the urban TFR fell to about half the rural TFR, and it remained at about that fraction when the large reduction in rural fertility began in 1970. Other differentials in fertility that are usually present in the first years of a major reduction were present in China in 1981: fertility was lower for more educated women and for women in higher occupational categories; the minority ethnic groups had much higher fertility than the rural Han majority.

Future Trends in Fertility. Further upward pressure on the birth rate in the late 1980s is built into the age distribution of the Chinese population, shown in Figure 2. Women in their early 20s in 1982 were born in 1958-61, a period of greatly reduced birth cohorts. In the next few years the very large birth cohorts of 1963-70 will be in the normal ages of first marriage and thereafter in the very fertile years soon after marriage.

Male/Female Birth Ratios. The large-scale fertility survey recorded ratios of male to female births that were very close to the worldwide normal ratio of about 106

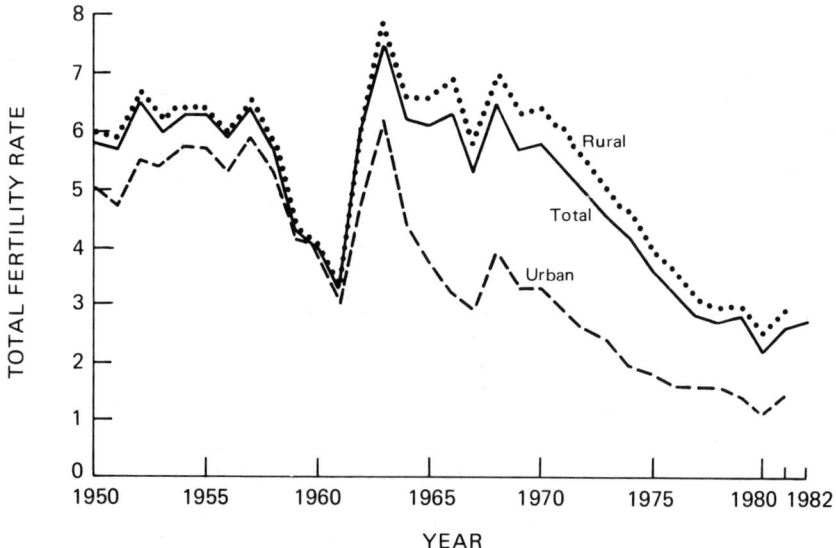

FIGURE 1 Total Fertility Rates for Urban and Rural Areas and for China, 1952-82: China

males per 100 females among first and second births in the rural population, but there were more than 112 males per 100 females for third- and higher-order births. The male/female ratio for urban births was somewhat higher (over 108) for first births, and much higher (about 118) among the small number (257) of births beyond the first. Experience in other populations is of slightly declining male/female ratios with birth order. Since stopping rules--no more births following a male--do not affect the male/female ratio and sex-selective abortion on a large scale does not seem possible in rural China, the explanation for the reported male/female birth ratios must be unreported higher-order female births. There may be a connection between failure to report a higher-order female birth in the survey and the occurrence of female infanticide, which has been widely reported (and deplored) in the Chinese press. Given the penalties imposed in the one-child campaign and the cultural preference for male births, higher-order female births are doubtless especially unwelcome.

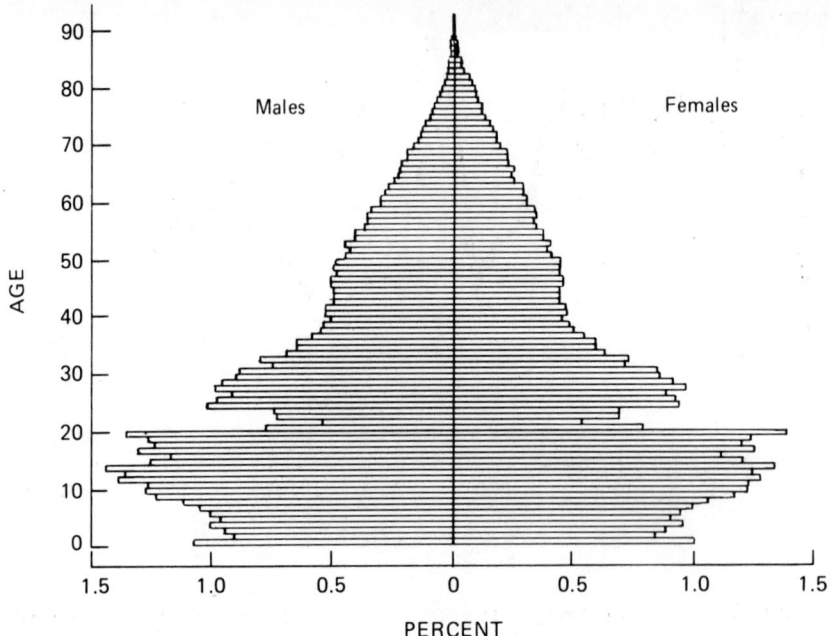

FIGURE 2   Age Pyramid of the Population, 1982:   China

Source: China, Population Census Office (1983:Table 19).

Life Expectancy. Average death rates by age for each sex in each intercensal interval can be calculated from census data and constructed numbers of births. From these death rates life tables are derived that show the average age at death that would result from the continued prevalence of the calculated intercensal average death rates. The expectation of life at birth increased from 42 for males and 46 for females in 1953-64 to 62 for males and 63 for females in 1964-68. This increase in less than two decades replicates the increase typical of six West European populations from 1870 to 1940. A life table was recently calculated for 1981 from deaths reported in the 1982 census. It shows a further increase in expectation of life at birth to 66 years for males and 69 for females.

Mortality Rates. Official figures on the annual number of deaths understate the true number by a greater proportion than the proportionate understatement of the number of births. It is possible to determine only the

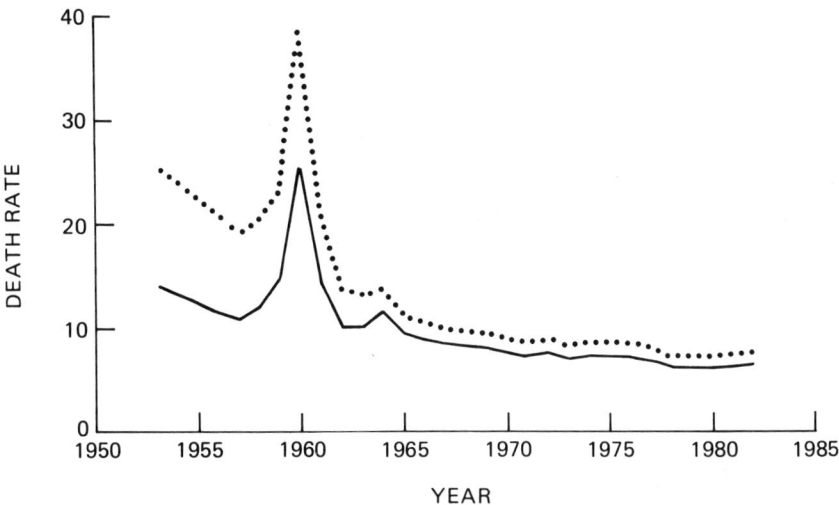

FIGURE 3 Death Rates (per 1,000) from Recorded Deaths (solid line) and Adjusted for Underreporting (dotted line), 1953-82: China

understatement of the total number of deaths for intercensal periods: about 38 percent of the deaths in 1953-64 were not recorded and about 16 percent of the deaths in 1964-82.

According to official sources, annual death rates (Figure 3) were about 15 per 1,000 in the early 1950s and declined to about 11 per 1,000 in 1957. There was an increase in death rates during the years of the Great Leap Forward and the ensuing crisis, with an officially listed peak rate of 25 per 1,000 in 1960. The death rate fell to 10 in 1963 as normal conditions were restored, then continued to decline to a rate between 6 and 7 per 1,000 in the late 1970s and early 1980s. When the intercensal aggregate shortfall in the number of deaths derived from official sources is allocated under an assumption of improving completeness after 1955 and constant completeness from 1964-82, the estimated death rate in the early 1950s is above 20, the peak death rate in 1960 is above 35, and the recent death rate is between 7 and 8 (rather than between 6 and 7). Excess deaths (those above a linear trend) from 1958-63 are about 16 million when based on the understated official figures and about 27 million when adjusted for understatement.

CHAPTER 1

INTRODUCTION

SCOPE OF THE REPORT

This report is a summary of fertility, nuptiality, and mortality in the People's Republic of China from the early 1950s to 1982. It is based largely on the single-year age distributions tabulated in the censuses of 1953, 1964, and 1982 (with some adjustment) and the detailed history of fertility and nuptiality collected in the large-scale 1982 survey of retrospective experience among 311,000 women aged 15-67. The survey was conducted by the State Family Planning Commission.

Much of the data presented here are taken from a special issue of the Chinese journal <u>Population and Economics</u>, published in 1983, which was devoted to detailed information about the fertility survey and its results. Some of the important features of the demography of China summarized in this report--such as the sequence of total fertility rates for each year since 1950--are simply reproduced from Chinese sources (in particular the special issue of <u>Population and Economics</u>). Other features, such as birth rates, completeness of official data on annual births and deaths, marital fertility rates by age and by duration of marriage, and intercensal life tables, were calculated for this report. The methods of calculation range from simple cumulation of fertility rates to newly invented methods of life-table construction from census data.

The report is intended as a summary of population trends and not as an account of their causes. It presents some treatment of what demographers call the proximate determinants of fertility, including an analysis of the influence of changes in nuptiality on fertility and inferences from the age structure of marital fertility about the probable absence or prevalence of contraceptive practice. It also comments on the most conspicuous features in the evolution of the population: the deficit of births and the excess of deaths in 1958-61 and the steep decline in fertility after 1970. However, the aim of the report remains demographic, to describe and analyze the population patterns in China.

BACKGROUND

With a population of just over 1 billion, China is the most populous country in the world. Its population is one-third larger than the second most populous country, India (with about 725 million in 1984). In area, however, China ranks only third; with 3.69 million square miles, it has almost exactly the same area as the United States, with 3.62 million square miles. China is geographically similar to the United States in other ways, too: its territory extends 3,100 miles from east to west, although its north-south distance of 3,500 miles is much greater than that of the United States. China also has extensive mountainous terrain and arid and semi-arid areas. In addition, the population of China, like that of the United States, is concentrated in the eastern part of the country (see map).

Located in East Asia, China has very long boundaries (17,445 miles), which include long borders with the Soviet Union and the Mongolian People's Republic to the north and northwest, borders with India, Pakistan, and Afghanistan for the most part to the west, and with the Socialist Republic of Vietnam to the south. A cross-section of the country would show a land mass lying at low altitudes in the east, rising to plateaus, and on to the mountains in the west, including the world's tallest, Mt. Everest at 28,911 feet. China's main lowlands, which include the Manchurian Plain, the North China Plain, the Middle and Lower Yangtse River, and the Southeastern Hills, cover about 386,000 square miles (Kaplan et al., 1980). These plains in the eastern and southeastern parts of the country contain large parts of the Chinese population. Through these plains flow some of China's major rivers, including Asia's longest, the 4,000-mile Yangtse, in central China and the 3,000-mile Yellow River in the north.

Despite a substantial expansion of China's urban population during the early twentieth century, the

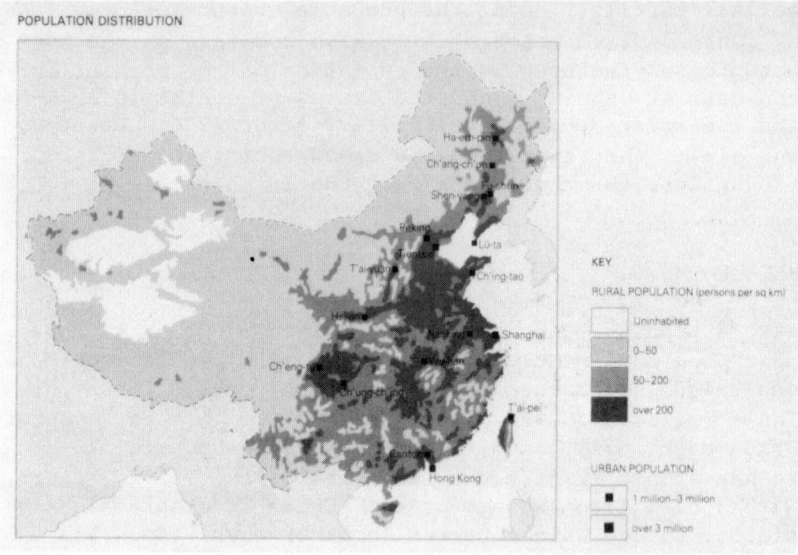

Source: Hook (1982:40).

country is still primarily rural; some four-fifths of the Chinese population reside in rural areas. The largest cities are Shanghai, on the southeastern coast, and Beijing, the capital, with 6.3 and 5.5 million inhabitants, respectively. Including the rural populations of the administrative districts, Shanghai has almost 12 million people and Beijing a little more than 9 million. The largest province is Sichuan, in the south, with more than 100 million people; thus, like Uttar Pradesh in India, if Sichuan Province were an independent nation, it would rank among the world's 10 most populous countries. Overall, China is divided into 22 provinces, 5 autonomous regions, and 3 municipalities.

Some 94 percent of the population of China consists of ethnic Chinese, known as Han (Kaplan et al., 1980). However, China is not unified linguistically: within the Chinese language, many mutually incomprehensible dialects are spoken, although the written Chinese language is uniform and can be understood by all. There are also a number of non-Chinese languages. The official spoken language of the People's Republic of China is "putonghua," meaning "standard speech," which is based on the northern Chinese dialect and is sometimes referred to in the West as Mandarin. China's 54 national minorities--60 million people-- live scattered across the half of China's land mass that they occupy. Speaking a variety of languages, they are encouraged by the authorities to maintain if not strengthen their cultural and linguistic identities.

CHAPTER 2

SOURCES AND QUALITY OF DATA

DATA SOURCES

The People's Republic of China had an enumerated total population in 1982 of more than 1 billion persons. The population has experienced dramatic recent reductions in birth and death rates, apparently surpassing the changes in any other very large less-developed country. These general features of the Chinese population had until recently been revealed in scattered information, such as travelers' reports, short news dispatches, and occasional sketchy official releases. Since the late 1970s, however, information on the population of China has been enriched by the sudden availability of a treasure of detailed demographic data--data relating both to the recent past and to the early years of the People's Republic.

Census and Fertility Survey Data

The 1982 Census and the 1982 Fertility Survey. The major sources of detailed information are two large data collection efforts that took place in 1982. The first of these was the 1982 census of population in which a field staff of 5.1 million enumerators counted a total of 1.008 billion people. The second effort was a sample survey conducted by the State Family Planning Commission, also in 1982. This survey obtained information about the complete childbearing and marriage histories of a sample of women aged 15-67. The households included in the survey had a population totalling more than 1 million. The survey included data on contraceptive practice, education, occupation, ethnicity, recent abortions, and possession of a one-child certificate.

The results were published (in Chinese) in a 176-page special issue of the journal Population and Economics.

Data from the 1953 and 1964 Censuses. The first modern census of China was conducted in 1953. Very limited results, such as the total population, were revealed in 1954, although fundamental details, such as numbers of persons classified by age and sex, remained unavailable outside of China. A second census took place in 1964; the mere fact that it occurred was not generally known until some years later, and again no details were released. Within the past two years, however, the most essential demographic information--the number of persons of each sex classified by single years of age--from these two censuses has been published. The Ministry of Statistics has also recently published the Statistical Yearbook for 1983 with hundreds of tables, including annual birth and death rates since 1950.

It is now possible to piece together from the newly available information the history of the population of the People's Republic of China from 1950 to 1982 with much more accuracy and more detail than has been possible until now. Indeed, as the following pages show, the accuracy and fineness of detail of the information about the Chinese population now exceed the accuracy and detail of what is known about almost every other less-developed country in the world.

Independence of the Data Sources

The various quantitative comparisons presented in the following pages convey a very surprising degree of consistency among numbers derived from the censuses of 1953, 1964, and 1982 and from the large-scale fertility survey. Some demographers and statisticians have suggested that the consistency of the data results from a lack of independence of the sources and is not convincing evidence of accuracy of the data. This possibility arises because China has a nationwide, comprehensive registration system. Each community maintains a register of the population in which there is a listing of the de jure population, to which an addition is made for each birth and legal in-migrant and a deletion is made for each death and legal out-migrant. The registration system also includes the maintenance of a household book containing a listing of the de jure members of each household. The 1982 census involved a preliminary nationwide updating of the registers in each community, and the registers and the household books played a part in the census itself. The fertility survey, which was conducted about 2 months after the census, used the census as the frame for its 1/1,000 sample and checked the roster of each household included in the sample against the census listing. The hypothesis that consistency may not imply accuracy derives from the possibility that the censuses (and perhaps the survey) were simply readings of the registers. If so, the mechanics of maintaining a register would guarantee that persons listed in 1964 and still alive in 1982 have a consistent age and that, on a national level (with inconsequential international migration), the change in the number listed in a cohort must be consistent with the deletions made as a result of recorded deaths. If the number of children born to a given woman is copied from the register, the number recorded in the 1982 census and the number listed in the sample survey might be the same without being correct.

There are two reasons for rejecting the hypothesis that consistency may not imply accuracy. The first is that the procedures followed in the 1982 census and survey, as published, involved much more than checking the registers. For the census, there was extensive preparation, pretesting, and postenumerative checking along with the actual census. It is also of note that the census was conducted with substantial technical and financial assistance from the United Nations. The census was closely tied to the registers, but only after extensive updating and verification; individual data were verified by the person in question. For the 1/1,000-sample fertility survey, the published descriptions of the procedures specified face-to-face interviews for the detailed marriage and fertility histories.

The second reason for rejecting the hypothesis is that the annual numbers of births derived from a combination of census-based estimates of numbers of women each year and survey-based retrospective data on fertility rates are quite different from official records of the annual number of births. In other words, the fertility histories are in wide disagreement with official data on births and so cannot have been derived from the registers.

Characteristics of the 1982 Census and Fertility Survey

Procedures of the 1982 Census. Li Chengrui, the director of the State Statistical Bureau and head of the National Population Census Office, has described the procedures of the 1982 census in detail (Li 1983a and 1983b). The procedures included pretests of the census in successive stages, beginning with a pretest conducted by the central government and extending to pretests in each of China's 2,741 counties, covering a total of more than 25 million people. In addition, the register of the population was updated before the census. Li summarizes these procedures (1983a:337):

> First, from the beginning of 1981 through March 1982, household registration was updated. In a sense, this amounted to a precensus check. During this period, more than 5.7 million household registration personnel, statistical personnel, and other basic-level cadres were mobilized to update household registration throughout the country. They conducted a systematic investigation through household interviews and found and corrected errors: 6.1 double registrations per thousand and 5.4 omissions per thousand. Second, prior to the formal enumeration on 1 July 1982, the enumerators arrived at their census districts and conducted a further investigation. They checked household by household for the "five types of persons" identified in the "Census statute" manual. During this procedure, further errors were found and corrected. Based on the information from a subset of areas, double registrations were found to amount to 3 per thousand population and omissions to 2.5 per thousand. Third, after the conclusion of the census enumeration, 10-20 days were spent rechecking household by household and person by person all the census questionnaires. Some errors were again found and corrected. Based on the information from a subset of areas, during the recheck, double countings of 0.1 per thousand and omissions of 0.2 per thousand were found and corrected.

Following these precensus and census procedures, there was a post-enumeration survey (Li, 1983a:338):

. . . the population census offices of the provinces, municipalities, and autonomous regions first selected, by multistage random sampling, 972 production teams and resident groups (a total of 187,362 persons according to the census) as the survey units. The provincial, prefectural, and county-level offices then selected persons who were of higher educational level and were conscientious and responsible in their work to undergo special training to become sample enumerators. They conducted the postenumeration survey in the selected sample units household by household and then compared the figures obtained with the figures of the original census enumeration. When errors were found, a second check was made before the data were corrected. Based on the stipulations, the census personnel who originally carried out the census enumeration in these production teams and resident groups were not selected as sample survey enumerators . . . . The sample check mentioned above shows a net overcount of 0.15 per thousand.

On the specific issue of the dependence of the census on the register, Li writes that the census included (1983a:339-340):

1. De jure population: 990,658,313

2. Persons who lived in the local area for more than one year but whose residence is registered elsewhere: 6,364,518

3. Persons who have lived less than one year in the locality but have left their place of registered residence for more than one year: 210,322

4. Persons who are living in the locality but whose residence registration is still pending: 4,754,602

5. Persons who originally lived in the locality but are working or studying abroad and have no residence registration: 56,930

The population of types 2 through 5 totals 11,386,372. These are persons who are not included in the local household registration books. The 4.75 million persons whose household registration is still pending have not been omitted from the census enumeration. They are listed as the fourth type and are included in the census population total. The figures given above are sufficient evidence that the population census is absolutely not a repetition of the household registration.

Features of the 1982 Fertility Survey. The large-scale survey of fertility conducted by the State Family Planning Commission in September 1982 (described in Xiao, 1983), had a reference date of July 1, the same date as the census. The sample frame was the census listing itself. It was a stratified self-weighting cluster sample, covering all households in 815 areas: 732 rural production brigades and 83 urban residents' committees. The total population in the survey was a little more than 1 million, involving a sampling fraction of about 1/1,000. The choice of such a very large sample size was based on the calculated number of respondents required to yield 95 percent confidence limits for the peak single-year age-specific fertility rates that would differ by only 5 percent from the rate calculated from the sample, after allowance for the greater variance in a cluster sample than in a simple random sample.[1] Because the sample was so large, estimates of age-specific fertility rates and rates of first marriage by single years of age extending back into the 1950s have remarkably low sampling variability. The estimated annual total number of births in China (and the associated crude birth rates and total fertility rates) are derived from the reported numbers of births in the sample, which range from about 15,000 for each year in the 1950s to more than 20,000 for 1981. The sampling standard deviation of such large numbers is no more than about 1 percent.

The survey had two parts, the survey of the de jure population to establish the composition of the households included in the sample and the detailed survey encompassing a variety of information about "qualified women"--all women aged 15-67. Data on the de jure population was copied from the results of the census, with verification of changes that might have taken place since July 1 using sources in the local areas (presumably the registers plus local informants). But great emphasis was put on the requirement that the survey of qualified women should be conducted by face-to-face interviews. The instructions on obtaining information in these interviews were explicit and detailed. They included specifications that all ages shall be entered in completed years and all dates in the solar calendar. An explanation of the relations among animal symbols, Chinese ages, solar ages in completed years, and solar and lunar calendars was included.

QUALITY OF DATA

Data By Single Years of Age

   Consistency of the Census Age Distributions. Figure 4 shows the proportion of women surviving from one census to the next classified by single years of age at the earlier census: the survival ratios are for 1953 to 1964 and 1964 to 1982. Also shown in Figure 4 are survival ratios extracted from a life table expressing the proportion that would survive from birth to each age in a hypothetical cohort subject to the average mortality rate at each age for the intercensal interval.^{2} The surprising feature of the single-year survival ratios calculated directly from the censuses is that there is so little irregularity. In most censuses the reported age distribution is distorted by what demographers call age-heaping, a tendency for too many persons to be reported at ages that respondents favor (usually ages ending in 0 or 5). However, because most intercensal intervals are either 5 or 10 years, the effect of age-heaping on survival ratios is usually dampened because preferred ages (e.g., 30 and 40) are in both numerator and denominator of the ratios. In China the intercensal intervals are 11 years and 18 years, but the survival ratios show almost no effect of age-heaping: from 1953 to 1964 the survival ratios for women aged 30, 35, 40, 45, 50, and 60 in 1953 are slightly too low (a favored age is in the denominator) and ratios at 29, 39, and 49 are slightly too high (a favored age is in the numerator), but the effect is very small. The high survival ratio from age 0 in 1953 to age 11 in 1964 is almost certainly the result of an undercount of infants under age 1 in 1953, possibly caused by age misstatement that inflates the number at age 1, leading to too low a survival ratio for this cohort. Other defects in the data are indicated

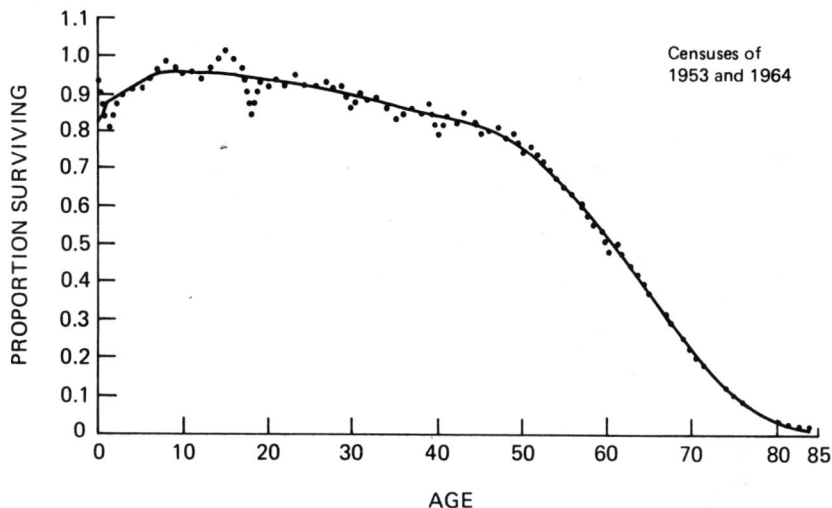

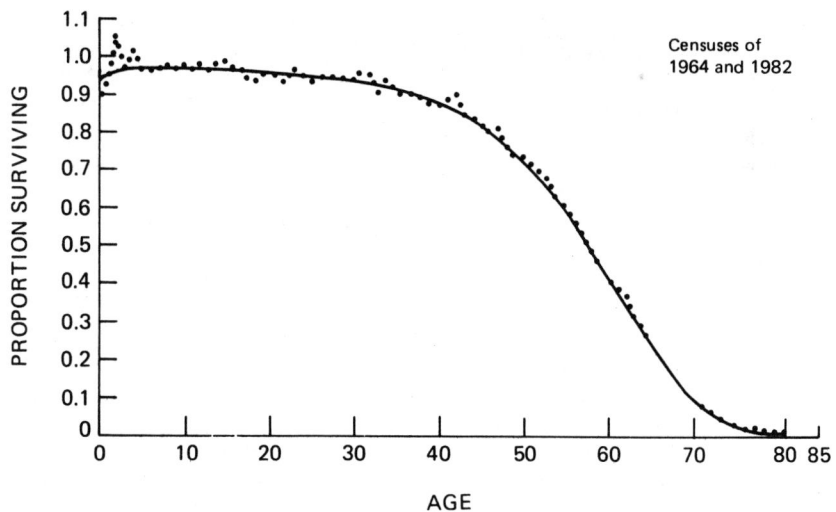

FIGURE 4 Proportion of Females Surviving Between Successive Censuses for Each Age (solid line is proportion derived from intercensal life table, dotted line is ratio taken directly from the census enumerations): China

by survival ratios above 1.0 at ages 2 and 4 in 1964-82
and at age 15 in 1953-64.

The limited fluctuations in the survival ratios
indicate highly uniform completeness of coverage by age
and extremely limited age misreporting. That very
accurate information about age can be obtained from a
Chinese population is well known. The reason is a
cultural one. People of East Asian culture (Chinese,
Japanese, Korean, etc.) almost universally know their
date of birth, even when illiterate, usually in terms of
the animal year of birth (in a cycle of 12 animals and 5
different qualities for each animal, a complete cycle
that repeats every 60 years) and the lunar month.
Because of this knowledge, if age is determined through a
question asking the date of birth, followed by use of a
formula that converts the animal year and lunar month to
a Western date, age can be determined with precision.
Evidently, such a procedure was used in all three
censuses.

<u>Consistency of Census and Fertility Survey Data</u>. The
data collected and tabulated from the large-scale fertility survey conducted by the Ministry of Family
Planning in 1982 are even more remarkable than the census
data in their internal consistency. The published tables
include rates of childbearing by single years of age and
single calendar years for women aged 15-49 for the years
from 1950 to 1981. Analogous rates of first marriage by
age are also included in the publication. These rates
are derived directly from the births and marriages
reported in the survey; because the dates of events are
accurately reported, the age of each woman at the time of
marriage and of each birth is readily determined.

The listing of birth rates by age of woman makes it
possible to construct an annual series of the total
number of births in China for each calendar year from
1950 to 1981. In order to construct that series, the
number of women by single years of age from 15 to 50 in
each calendar year is calculated by interpolating between
the number in each cohort recorded in two censuses. That
is, one can determine with good precision (on the
assumption that the censuses are accurate) the number of
persons at age 15 in 1954 by subtracting from the number
14 in 1953 one-eleventh of the decrease in this cohort
between its enumeration in 1953 at age 11 and its
enumeration in 1964 at age 25.[3] The number of births
that occurred in each year is then calculated by

multiplying the number of women at each age (determined through cohort interpolation of census data) by the age-specific rate of childbearing taken from the fertility survey and summing these births for all women aged 15-49. (The number of women classified by single years of age from 15-49 in each year appears in Table A-1. Tables that contain primarily raw data or large sets of calculated data are included in the appendix.) The numbers of births so calculated from 1951 to 1981 permit a sensitive test of the consistency of the fertility rates from the survey with the data on age distribution in the censuses of 1964 and 1982. For example, the number of persons at age 5 (i.e., between exact age 5.0 and exact age 6.0) in 1964 must equal the number born between July 1, 1958, and July 1, 1959, multiplied by the proportion who survived from birth to age 5.[4] The number of persons aged 23 in 1982 must equal the number at 5 in 1964 in this cohort multiplied by the proportion who survived from 1964 to 1982. Appropriate survival rates have been extracted from intercensal life tables derived from the censuses and the estimated numbers of births.

In short, there are two sets of numbers for the population classified by single years of age from 0 to 11 in 1964 and from 0 to 29 in 1982. One set is taken from the census and the other from estimated births and survival rates from the survey--the births calculated from retrospective fertility rates combined with interpolated numbers of women and the survival rates from intercensal life tables. In Figure 5 the two sets of numbers are compared. The agreement is extraordinary, especially since the reallocation of births from calendar year to fiscal year is necessarily only approximate and would be so even if the number of calendar-year births were exact.

Abnormal Ratios of Men to Women in Census and Survey Data

Omission of Males from the Census Age Distributions.
A systematic deficiency in the reported age and sex distributions in the Chinese censuses becomes evident when the ratio of men to women at each age is plotted. Such plots are shown in Figures 6 and 7. In each census it is apparent that the number of males in the young adult span--from 16 to 40 in 1953, from 16 to 24 in 1964, and from 16 to 23 in 1982--is too low, because of the

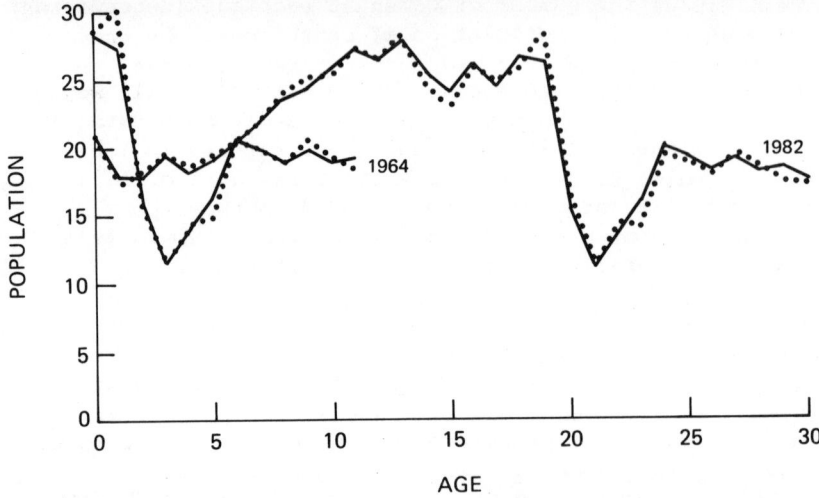

FIGURE 5 Number of Persons Under Age 30 in 1982 and Number of Persons Under Age 11 in 1964 (in millions) by Single Years of Age, as Projected (solid line) and as Enumerated in the Census (dotted line): China

omission of males, mostly those who are in the army. The 1982 census lists the number of males and females in the army, although without giving their ages. The number in the army is 4.2 million, of whom 109,000 are female. In 1953 the news release that reported the conduct of the census gave a population of 574.2 million who were "directly enumerated," and an additional 8.4 million who were indirectly enumerated. The recently released single-year age distribution for 1953 totals only 567.4 million. The 6.8 million difference between the total for which an age distribution is released and the total that was directly enumerated may be taken as the number of persons in military service. Ostensibly the 1964 census included the army, but it is evident from the ratio of males to females in the ages of principal military service that a large number of males at these ages were omitted. In 1953 and 1982 an adjusted age distribution was constructed by allocating the known or estimated number of persons in the armed services age by age, using a rough estimate of the ratio of males to females at each age based on the ratio at ages prior to the range of military service and the ratio at ages above

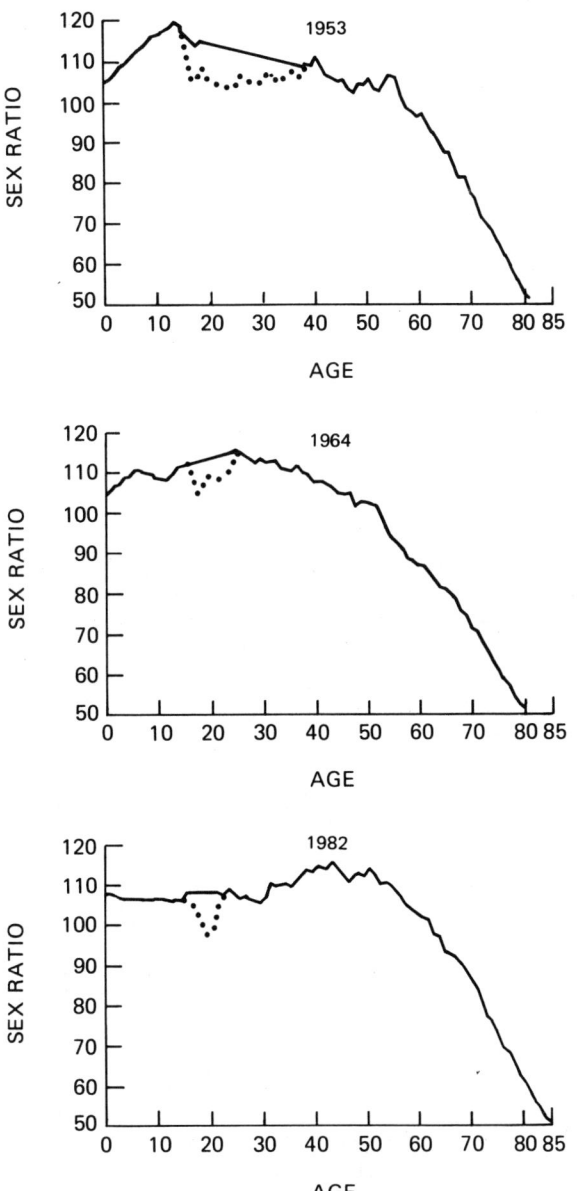

FIGURE 6 Sex Ratio (males per 100 females) by Single Years of Age (dotted line represents original data, solid line includes estimates of males in armed services), 1953, 1964, and 1982: China

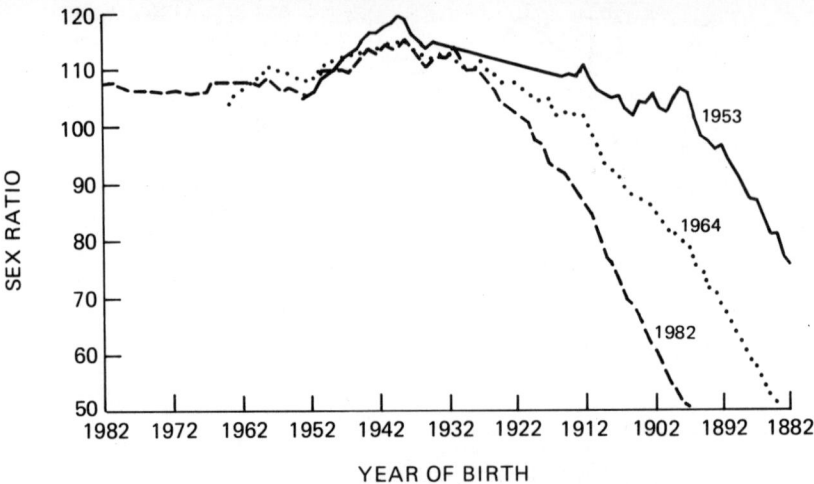

FIGURE 7 Sex Ratio (males per 100 females) by Year of Birth for Censuses of 1953, 1964, and 1982 (estimated number of males in armed services included): China

Note: Year of birth refers to 12 months calculated as of January 1 of given date.

this range. A similar procedure was used to add males at ages 16-23 in 1964, but without a listed total in the army from official data. (The adjusted age distributions are given in Table A-2.)

A remarkable feature of the male/female ratios in the three censuses is the increase in the ratio with age in all three censuses, from a moderate ratio for the cohorts born around 1951 to a ratio of 115 males or more per 100 females for those born in 1940, and the continued high ratio of males to females for cohorts born still earlier. The normal expectation in a population not gaining or losing significantly from migration is that the male/female ratio will be highest at birth (at about 106 males per 100 females) and decline more or less monotonically with age because of the general prevalence of higher male than female mortality rates. Such a declining male/female ratio occurs at the older ages in the Chinese censuses. The anomalous increase seen for the birth cohorts of 1951-52 back to the cohorts born about 1940 in all three censuses implies that those born before about 1952 experienced higher female than male mortality, contrary to the usual greater viability of females. Another remarkable feature of the ratio of males to females is the precipitous drop in this ratio at older ages, especially the decline in the male/female between 1953 and 1964 for older cohorts. The decline in the proportion male within the same cohort by as much as 25 percent in 11 years suggests an extraordinary excess mortality for males.

Male/Female Ratios in the Fertility Survey. There are two anomalous features of the ratio of males to females in the 1/1,000-sample fertility survey. The first is that the ratio of males to females in the de jure population was 102.8 males per 100 females, compared to 106.8 for the census (Liu and Li, 1983). The standard deviation for the ratio in a sample of 1 million is about 2/1,000, so that the difference cannot be from sampling variation. The difference is mostly from ages 20 to 60; in each five-year age interval the male/female ratio in the census is at least three points higher--and as much as nine points higher at ages 35-39. In view of the consistencies of several kinds in the fertility histories (see below), it may be conjectured that less care was taken in establishing the de jure population of the households than in collecting the detailed marriage and fertility histories.

The second anomaly is puzzling information in a table that lists the number of male and female births in 1981 by sex and birth order in the rural and urban populations. The puzzle is an increase in the male/female ratio as birth order increases, in both rural and urban populations. In most populations the ratio of male to female births is about 1.06, and in well-recorded vital statistics there is only a slight difference in the male/female ratio of births at different birth orders--a difference in the direction of a very small reduction in the ratio as birth order rises. In the Chinese fertility survey the ratio of male to female births in the rural population is 1.046 for first births, 1.069 for second births, and 1.124 for births of third and higher order. In the urban population, the ratio is 1.085 for first births and 1.178 for births of second and higher order. (There were only 257 urban births above the first order reported for 1981.) The male/female ratio of 1.055 among rural births of first and second order in 1981 is very close to the normal ratio, but there is a marked increase in the ratio with birth order—above first-order births in the urban population and above second- order births in the rural population. The reality of this increase can be challenged on the basis that it may be the effect of mere random variation in the male/female ratio when the number of births is small. The standard deviation of the ratio of male to female births caused by stochastic variation is approximately $2\sqrt{n}$ when n is the total number of births. Since there were only 257 urban births of second or higher order, the ratio of 1.178 for higher-order urban births differs by less than one standard deviation from a normal ratio of 1.06; the possibility that the high male/female ratio occurred by chance cannot in this instance be ruled out. However, the male/female ratio of 1.124 for rural births of third or higher order (there were 5,957 such births reported) is 2.47 standard deviations above 1.06. It is scarcely possible that the uniformly higher male/female of urban births and the regular increase in the ratio with birth order in both rural and urban births are the results of sampling quirks.

The relatively high male/female ratios in higher-order births might be the result of simple underreporting of higher-order females births in the survey. It is understandable that a higher-order birth that occurred contrary to the one-child campaign would be unregistered because the parents would want to conceal such a birth. Given the cultural preference for males, local officials might be sympathetic in registering a higher-order male birth and join in keeping unregistered a higher-order female birth. Comparison of births reported in the survey for 1981 and registered births shows that more than 3 million births in that year were not registered. It is possible that the much more complete reporting in the survey still omitted the births of surviving female children.[5] Sex-selective abortion is not yet technologically feasible and certainly not in the rural areas. A possibility that remains is unreported sex-selective infanticide. Such a practice would likely be unreported in an official survey and might rise with birth order because of the increasing penalties accompanying higher-order births. There are many reports of female infanticide in the Chinese press; it is mentioned as a possible explanation of the high male/female ratio of the higher-order births by Liu and Li (1983).

Official Data on Births and Deaths

Official Figures of Annual Numbers of Births. As noted above, the age-specific fertility rates constructed from the fertility survey can be combined with the calculated number of females by single years of age to produce estimates of the annual number of births. The annual number of births so constructed can be compared with the annual number taken from official sources, presumably based on the number of births registered (see Table 1). The estimated number exceeds the official number with only one exception. The ratio of the official figures to the constructed figures is a valid estimate of the completeness of the official figures since the estimated figures are very consistent with the numbers counted at each age in the censuses. Completeness of official reporting in each year is shown in Figure 8, together with a three-year moving average of completeness.

The moving average is useful to show the general trend of completeness of recording, free of large year-to-year fluctuations. There are two likely reasons for the fluctuations. One reason is imperfect conversion of date of birth in the fertility survey to the western (solar) calendar if the year of birth was reported in the Chinese (lunar) calendar. According to the Chinese calendar, years of 12 lunar months are interspersed, irregularly, with years of 13 lunar months. If year of birth was reported according to the Chinese calendar, there would be too many births reported in the 13-month years and too few in the 12-month years. The result would be understated estimates of completeness of recording in 13-month years and overstated estimates in the other years. In Figure 8 the 13-month years are labeled; it is clear that too many births were reported in those years. The second reason for large year-to-year fluctuations in the sequence of estimated completeness of reporting births is a possible tendency to report births in the year following their occurrence. An unusually large degree of delayed reporting might reduce estimated completeness in one year and increase it in the next. The most puzzling estimate of completeness of reporting is the high estimate for 1967 (more than 1.0 before correction for the effect of the use of a lunar calendar). There may be some connection between this anomaly and the disruption that resulted from the Cultural Revolution, which had just begun.

TABLE 1 Annual Number of Births (in millions) from Official Figures and as Calculated from Fertility Rates in Survey and Interpolated Populations, and Estimated Completeness of Reporting, 1953-82: China

	Number of Births		
Year	Official	Calculated	Completeness of Reporting
1953	21.51	24.54	.877
1954	22.45	25.76	.877
1955	19.79	25.94	.763
1956	19.76	29.45	.808
1957	21.67	27.13	.799
1958	19.05	24.16	.788
1959	16.47	18.48	.892
1960	13.89	17.38	.799
1961	11.88	14.52	.818
1962	24.60	26.78	.918
1963	29.54	33.53	.881
1964	27.29	28.01	.974
1965	27.09	27.94	.968
1966	25.77	29.28	.880
1967	25.63	25.35	1.011
1968	27.57	31.48	.878
1969	27.15	28.68	.947
1970	27.36	29.98	.913
1971	25.67	29.07	.883
1972	25.66	27.49	.933
1973	24.63	26.14	.942
1974	22.35	25.26	.885
1975	21.04	22.70	.927
1976	18.54	21.64	.857
1977	17.87	19.97	.894
1978	17.45	19.96	.873
1979	17.27	20.95	.824
1980	17.99	17.74	.844
1981	17.46	21.05	.830
1982	(21.26)	(21.56)	

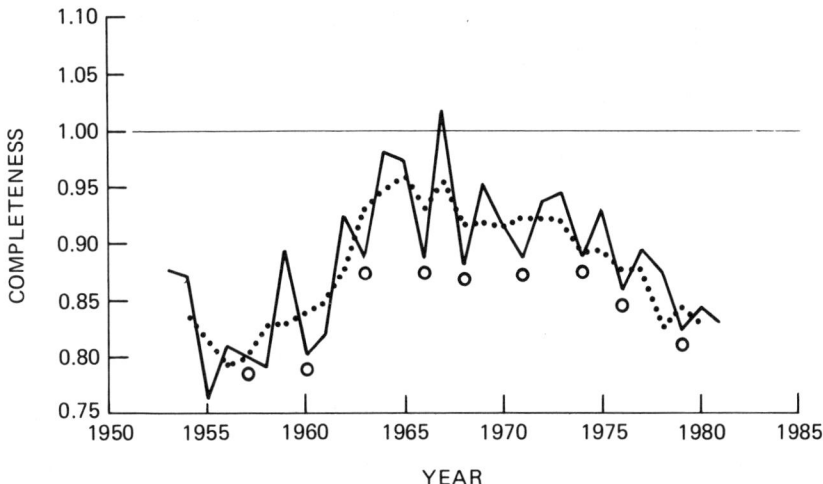

FIGURE 8 Completeness of Recording of Births (dotted line is 3-year moving average), 1953-81: China

Note: Circles designate years with 13 lunar months.

The moving average of completeness rises from about 80 percent in the mid-1950s to above 90 percent from 1963 to 1974; there is a decrease in completeness to less than 85 percent for years in the late 1970s. The official pressure for restriction of the number of births probably led to incomplete recording in those later years, both by parents fearful of penalties and by officials eager to meet targets.

Official Records of Death Rates. The completeness of death registration for each intercensal period as a whole can be estimated on the basis of the total population recorded in each census and the total number of births found to occur in each intercensal period. The difference between the total number of births between two censuses and the intercensal growth in population is the total number of deaths in that interval. The figure used for 1953 in these calculations includes the 8.4 million officially reported as indirectly enumerated; the 1964 figure includes an estimated 2.35 million young males omitted from the census, an estimate obtained by correcting understated ratios of males to females from age

16 to age 24; and the 1982 figure includes the official number in the armed service, whose ages were not reported. The number of deaths calculated in this way can be compared with the number implied by official figures for the population each year and with the annual death rate (State Statistical Bureau, 1983b). The calculations are as follows:

	Period	
	1953-64	1964-82
Calculated Births (millions)	265.4	448.6
Intercensal Increase in Population (millions)	114.3	311.3
Calculated Deaths (millions)	151.1	137.3
Official Number of Deaths (millions)	93.7	115.8
Completion of Recording of Deaths (percent)	0.620	0.843

The aggregate completeness of recording of deaths is 62.0 percent for 1953-64, and 84.3 percent for 1964-82. The degree of understatement, especially in the earlier period, is surprising, but it is hard to see how the omission of deaths could in fact have been much less. The consistency between the calculated annual births and the census enumerations by age was noted earlier; besides, it seems unlikely that respondents in the fertility survey overstated the number of births that had occurred to them. This possibility is especially remote because of the extraordinary agreement (mostly within 1 percent) between the number of children ever born by five-year age intervals constructed from the survey and the number reported by women in the same intervals in the 1982 census. The annual number of births estimated for the intercensal years incorporates the census populations as the source of the estimated number of women at each childbearing age, so that the birth estimates are necessarily consistent with the increasing population from one census to the next (if the fertility rates are correct). The other possible source of an overestimate of the omission of deaths in the official data is understatement of the intercensal increase in population--an understatement that would imply that the earlier census was a more complete count than the later one, which is unlikely.

Comparison of the total number of registered births with the estimated total for the same intercensal periods leads to an estimate of average completeness of birth registration of 84.2 percent in 1953-64 and 91.2 percent in 1964-82. If a large fraction of the omitted births were births soon followed by an infant death that also went unrecorded, much of the estimated underrecording of deaths would be accounted for. The estimated number of unrecorded births in 1953-64 is 41.9 million, and the estimated number of unrecorded deaths is 57.4 million; the corresponding numbers for 1963-82 are 40.4 million unrecorded births, and 21.5 million unrecorded deaths.

These calculations are sensitive to the relative completeness of enumeration in the census. For example, if the 1964 census was undercounted by 2 percent more than the other two censuses, the calculated intercensal births would be increased by about 1 percent, the 1953-64 increase in population would be augmented by 13.9 million, and the 1964-82 increase would be diminished by the same amount. The estimated completeness of death recording would then be 67 percent for 1953-64 and 74 percent for 1964-82.

In the analysis of mortality in Chapter 5, three other sources of data are used for comparative purposes. One is an epidemiological survey conducted throughout China in 1973-75 in which deaths by age and sex and an age distribution of the population were recorded; the second is another large-scale survey in 1978 covering a sample population of over 100 million, reported in System Engineering and Science Management (Beijing) February, 1980, and the third is a life table constructed from the deaths in 1981 recorded in the 1982 census.

Data on Children and Marriage

Consistency of Survey and Census Data on Number of Children Ever Born. In addition to the consistency test described above ("Consistency of Census and Fertility

Survey Data"), a second test of the consistency of the age-specific fertility rates derived from the fertility survey and the 1982 census provides further evidence of very precise data. The age-specific fertility rates presented in the report of the survey for calendar years of time are converted into estimated fertility rates for fiscal years (July 1 to June 30) by a simple arithmetic average of the rates in two consecutive years. The rate of childbearing for women aged 15 in 1977-78, plus the rate of those aged 16 in 1978-79, plus the rate of those aged 17 in 1979-80, plus the rate of those aged 18 in 1980-81, plus the rate of those aged 19 in 1981-82 equals the average number of children ever born to women reaching exact age 20 in the middle of 1982.[6] By an analogous summation the estimated number of children ever born to women of each exact age from 16 to 65 can be ascertained. Then the average number of lifetime births of women at conventional single-year age intervals (15-16, 16-17, etc.) can be obtained by averaging (but using the geometric mean for the number born to women below age 20, to allow for the nonlinearity of the increasing number of children ever born at the youngest ages). Finally, the average number of children ever born to women at age 15 can be multiplied by the number of 15-year-olds in the 1982 census; the sum of such products for ages 15 through 19 yields the total number of children ever born to women aged 15-19. In Table 2 the total number of children ever born to women by five-year age intervals from ages 15-19 to 55-59 as constructed by this procedure is compared with the total number of children ever born reported by women in these age intervals in the 1982 census. The degree of consistency is remarkable: at 15-19 and 20-24 the constructed number of children ever born is within 2 percent of the census number; above age 25 for every age interval the agreement is within 1 percent.

<u>Consistency Between Survival Rates of Cohorts and Proportion of Children Ever Born Reported as Surviving</u>. William Brass was the originator of a widely used system for estimating child mortality from the fraction of children reported as surviving among the children ever born to women at different ages (Brass, 1968; United Nations 1983). One estimates the fraction of births that occurred to women in each time interval before a census or survey and selects a mortality schedule (e.g., from model life tables) that would yield the reported

TABLE 2 Total Number of Children Ever Born to Women Classified in Five-Year Age Intervals, 1982: China

	Number of Children Ever Born (millions)		
Age of Women	From 10 Percent Sample Tabulation of Census	Constructed from Age-Specific Fertility Rates in Survey	Ratio: Survey/Census
15-19	0.873	.859	.984
20-24	15.29	15.08	.986
25-29	71.27	71.51	1.003
30-34	96.68	96.66	1.000
35-39	97.36	96.92	.996
40-44	104.67	104.00	.994
45-49	119.54	118.62	.992
50-54	109.42	109.03	.996
55-59	90.79	90.81	1.000

proportion surviving, given the time distribution of the births. If $c(a)$ is the proportion of the children ever born to women aged 25-29 who were born "a" years before the census or survey and $p(a)$ is the fraction of these children surviving from birth to the census or survey date, then the overall proportion surviving, P, necessarily equals $\int_0^\omega c(a)p(a)da$, when ω is the time between the earliest birth and the census date. Brass' technique is to estimate $c(a)$ from information about the fertility history of the women in question, and by trial and error (or the logical equivalent) to select a survival function, $p(a)$, that is consistent with the reported proportion surviving among the children ever born to these women.

In the 10 percent sample tabulation of the 1982 census there are tables listing the number of children ever born alive, and the number of children surviving, for women classified in five-year age intervals from 15-19 to 55-59. For each age group of women the fraction of the children they have borne that were born in each year prior to the census can be determined from the age-specific fertility rates recorded in the fertility survey (which had the same effective date as the census). Consider women at exact age 20 in mid-1982: The births they had at age 19 occurred in 1981-82, those they had at age 18 in 1980-81, at 17 in 1979-80, at 16 in 1978-79, and at 15 in 1977-78. From age-specific fertility rates, one can calculate the fraction of births to those women that occurred at specified single-year periods in the past. A similar calculation can be made for women at exact age 18 in 1982; an average of the fraction in each period for those aged exactly 18 and those aged exactly 19 is a robust estimate of the fraction born in each period to women who were 18-19. Combining such calculations for women aged 15-16, 16-17, 17-18, 18-19, and 19-20, one obtains an estimate of the fraction of the children born alive by women 15-19 whose birth occurred in 1981-82, the fraction whose birth occurred in 1980-81, etc. The proportional distribution of births by fiscal year before the censuses, calculated in this manner, is shown for each group of women from 15-19 to 50-54 in Table A-3.

The distributions in Table A-3 are single-year interval tabulations of the function $c(a)$ that is combined with the proportion surviving, $p(a)$, in the Brass equation: proportion surviving = $\int_0^\omega c(a)p(a)da$. It would be possible to try different cohort survival functions and choose which among a set of possible $p(a)$ functions is consistent with the proportion surviving reported in the census. Instead, a value of $p(a)$ for each birth cohort is taken from Table 3, in which the survival ratio from birth in a given year to enumeration in 1982 has been calculated as the ratio of $(_1N_a)_{82}/B(82-a)$, where $(_1N_a)_{82}$ is the number enumerated at age a to a + 1 in 1982, and B(82-a) is the number of fiscal-year births a years before mid-1982. The fiscal-year births are based, in turn, on interpolated populations of women of childbearing age and age-specific fertility rates for each year in the past from the fertility survey. In other words, instead of using the Brass equation to chose a $p(a)$ function from some arbitrary set of such functions, the equation is used to calculate the proportion of children surviving among the children ever born to women in each five-year age interval. The determination of proportion surviving uses a $c(a)$ for each age group of women derived from their fertility histories and a $p(a)$ for each cohort derived from the census enumeration and estimated births. The result is a set of <u>constructed</u> proportions surviving (based primarily on the fertility histories from the survey) that can be compared with the proportions <u>reported</u> in the census. The comparison is shown in Table 4.

TABLE 3 Estimated Fiscal Year Births, 1951-52 to 1981-82, Number Recorded in Corresponding Cohort in 1982, and Proportion Surviving: China

Age in 1982	Year of Birth	Fiscal Year Births (millions)	Number in Census (millions)	Proportion Surviving
0-1	1981-82	21.71	20.81	.959
1-2	1980-81	18.93	17.38	.918
2-3	1979-80	19.06	18.27	.959
3-4	1978-79	20.87	19.62	.940
4-5	1977-78	19.63	18.63	.949
5-6	1976-77	20.67	19.42	.939
6-7	1975-76	22.07	20.42	.926
7-8	1974-75	24.00	21.78	.907
8-9	1973-74	25.86	24.03	.929
9-10	1972-73	26.73	25.09	.938
10-11	1971-72	28.33	25.22	.891
11-12	1970-71	29.88	27.33	.915
12-13	1969-70	29.09	26.50	.911
13-14	1968-69	30.68	28.24	.920
14-15	1967-68	28.28	24.52	.867
15-16	1966-67	26.72	22.74	.851
16-17	1965-66	28.10	25.97	.892
17-18	1964-65	27.11	24.78	.915
18-19	1963-64	31.61	25.78	.815
19-20	1962-63	32.38	28.59	.883
20-21	1961-62	19.46	16.59	.852
21-22	1960-61	14.28	11.20	.784
22-23	1959-60	17.57	14.51	.826
23-24	1958-59	21.08	14.29	.678
24-25	1957-58	26.69	19.45	.729
25-26	1956-57	25.97	18.89	.727
26-27	1955-56	24.88	17.92	.720
27-28	1954-55	26.20	19.67	.751
28-29	1953-54	25.00	18.62	.747
29-30	1952-53	25.52	17.49	.685
30-31	1951-52	24.44	17.36	.711

The agreement between constructed and reported proportions surviving is remarkably close for women aged 25-29 to 40-44. The deviation at the youngest age intervals (under age 25) is explained by the fact that survival of children is not independent of age of mother. The construction for women aged 15-19, for example, uses the estimated survival ratio for all births in 1981-82, 1980-81, and 1979-80; but in fact the infant

TABLE 4 Proportion of Children Surviving Among Children Ever Born Alive to Women Aged 15-19 to 50-54, 1982: China

Age of Woman	Constructed from Fertility Survey	Reported in Census
15-19	.949	.920
20-24	.944	.938
25-29	.940	.936
30-34	.927	.925
35-39	.903	.903
40-44	.876	.877
45-49	.826	.843
50-54	.764	.801

mortality rate among first births and among children born to very young women is higher than the general infant mortality rate. The deviation at ages 45-49 and 50-54 may be caused either by a slight overstatement of proportion surviving in the census reports by older women or by a slight overestimate of births in the early 1950s (for which the fertility rates of older women are not based on retrospective data because of the age limit of 67 years in the survey). Another possibility is that at higher ages differential mortality among mothers may have left respondents with relatively favorable mortality experience and with children who also had higher than average survival rates.

The basic agreement between reported and constructed proportions attests to the probable validity of the cohort survival ratios--not to the validity of individual ratios, but to the average survival of groups of cohorts. Individual survival ratios can be in error because the estimation of fiscal-year births involves an arbitrary element and because of slight deviations of the reported time of birth caused by incomplete adjustment from the lunar to the solar calendar.

<u>Consistency of First-Marriage Rates and Marital Status Data</u>. When the single-year rates of first marriage are cumulated for persons aged 15 in year t, 16 in $t + 1$, and 17 in $t + 2$, the resultant sum is the proportion of ever-married women at exact age 18 at the end (December

31) of year t + 2. By such cumulations the proportions of ever-married women at age a and a + 1 at the beginning and end of each year can be determined; the average of these four numbers is an estimate of the proportion of ever-married women in the middle of the year of those between ages a and a + 1.

The proportion of ever-married women aged 15-35 from 1950 to 1981 calculated in this way is shown in Table A-4, which also lists the proportion of ever-married women in 1982 as ascertained in the de jure listing of households. The series of constructed proportions in 1980 and 1981 are very similar through age 19 to the reported proportion in 1982; above age 20 the increase in proportion married from 1980 to 1981 and from 1981 to 1982 reflects the rise in first-marriage rates.

The proportion of ever-married women by age are tabulated at 15-19 and by single year of age from 20 to 29 in the 10 percent tabulation of the 1982 census. For women aged 22 to 29 the proportion ever-married in the survey differs by at most 0.005 from the proportion in the census, but for women aged 15-19 the proportion is 2 percent greater in the survey (.062 compared with .042), and at 20 and 21 the proportion ever married in the survey exceeds the proportion ever married in the census by 1.2 percent and 0.9 percent, respectively. In the survey the enumerators were instructed to include as married those for whom no marriage certificate had been issued but who were recognized as being married by the family and the society (Xiao, 1983). This explainable difference is further evidence that data for the census and survey were not simply copied from the same register.

Quality of Data: Summary

A number of results have emerged from this examination of the quality of Chinese population data. The most important is the good but not perfect accuracy of the fertility and marriage information collected in the large-scale fertility survey. The retrospective fertility data provide the basis for constructing an annual series of births and birth rates, which is an addition to the published total fertility rates. The number of births in this series exceeds the number of births listed in official sources by a substantial margin; the fertility data could not have been copied from registers. In fact, the synchronism of low points in the ratio (of the number of officially reported births to the number of calculated births) with years containing 13 lunar months is evidence that the fertility histories were obtained from respondents. In addition, there is a slight systematic bias in the time sequence of total fertility rates--which are too high in years with 13 lunar months. Further evidence of the independence of the survey from the register (and the census) is found in the higher proportion of ever-married women in the survey than in the census at young ages, a natural result of instructions in the survey to include married persons whose marriages had not been registered.

The consistency of cumulative fertility in the survey with the number of children ever born in the census is so close that independence is hard to believe. Nevertheless, there is no doubt, given the explicit nature of the instructions, the overreporting of births in 13-month years, and the excess of births reported in the survey in comparison with the official reports, that the detailed fertility history was in fact obtained by interviews with the qualified respondents. The interviewers might have had access to the total number of children ever born that the respondent listed on the census and might have probed for an omitted birth when the total number reported was less than the census response. But if the detailed fertility history yielded one more birth than the census, the interviewer would have been unlikely to scratch one birth from the survey form and it would not have been impossible to add one to the census. Moreover, the latter would have an inconsequential effect on the census results since the survey was a 1/1,000 sample.

The congruence of the proportions dead among children ever born constructed from the calculated birth sequence and the proportions dead reported in the census is powerful evidence of the validity of the birth sequence. It supports, indeed, the approximately equal coverage of the 1964 and 1982 censuses since the constructed survival rates for children born to women aged 40-44 are heavily weighted by the births estimated around 1964. If the 1964 census had been undercounted relative to 1982, the number of births around 1964 would have been underestimated, the survival rates to 1982 would be too high, and the constructed proportion surviving for women aged 40-44 would exceed the reported proportion.

With some minor exceptions, then, the fertility and nuptiality information taken from the census and survey can be accepted as of high quality; as such, they provide the basis for a valid history of recent trends in China.

CHAPTER 3

MARRIAGE IN CHINA SINCE 1950

The 1/1,000-sample survey conducted in 1982 by the Ministry of Family Planning collected retrospective data on marriages as well as on births. The report of the survey includes tables listing rates of first marriage by single years of age (the number of first marriages in a single-year age interval relative to the number of women in the interval) for each calendar year from 1949 to 1981. It also provides the calculated mean age at first marriage and the total first marriage rate for each year from 1940 to 1982 (Zhao and Yu, 1983). The total first-marriage rate for a given year is the sum of the single-year age-specific rates of first marriage. It equals the proportion that would ever marry in a hypothetical cohort subject to the marriage rates of the year in question.

PROPORTION EVER-MARRIED WOMEN AND THE FIRST-MARRIAGE RATE

Actual cohorts of women in China achieve very close to 100 percent entry into marriage, as is evident in the proportion of women ever married by single years of age in 1982--more than 98 percent at ages 29 and 30 and more than 99 percent at every age over 30. The annual total rate of first marriage has nevertheless differed from unity in most years, often substantially. It reached a low of .74 in 1959, during the Great Leap Forward, a high of 1.19 in 1962, as the economy and society recovered from the Great Leap Forward and the "bitter years" of 1960-61; and fell again to .71 and .73 in 1965 and 1966, at the beginning of the Cultural Revolution (see Figure 9). The lowest point of .64 was reached in 1973, in the midst of a rapid rise in the mean age at first marriage. From

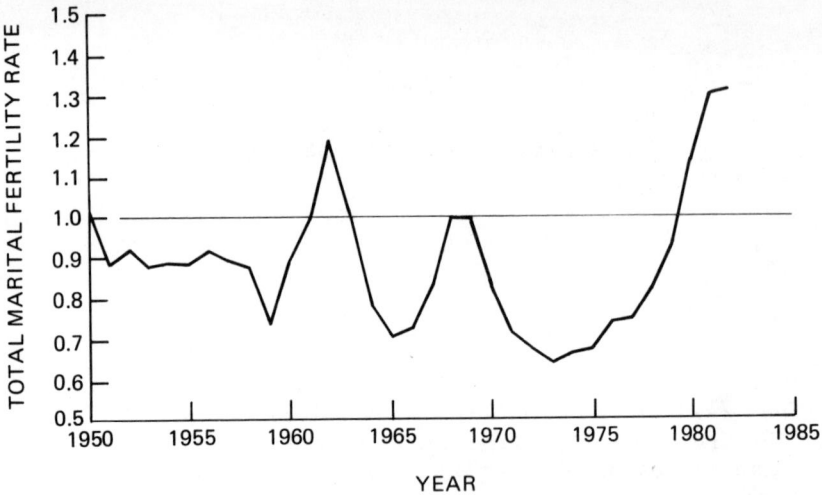

FIGURE 9 Total Female First-Marriage Rate (sum of first marriage frequencies), 1950-82: China

1971 to 1979, while mean age at first marriage was increasing from 20.29 to 23.05--an addition of almost one-third of a year each year--the total first-marriage rate was below 1.0 despite the ultimate achievement of nearly 100 percent ever married within each cohort. In 1980 the total first-marriage rate reached 1.14, higher than in any previous year except 1962; in 1981 and the first 6 months of 1982 it rose to a new high above 1.30, a boom in marriages that caused increased births in 1981 and 1982 and will have a continued upward effect on births in 1983.

There are two reasons for differences from unity in the annual total first-marriage rate even when every cohort experiences a proportion ever married very close to 100 percent. One reason is a temporary deficit in the number of marriages in years when social disruption prevents marriages that otherwise would occur and an excess in the number of marriages in the period of recovery from such episodes (for example, the deficit in 1959 and the excess in 1962). The second reason for high or low total rates of first marriage is a change in the mean age at which cohorts marry. When the mean age at marriage of a cohort falls, the total marriage rate rises above 1.0 because the marriages of older and younger

women, which would have occurred sequentially with
constant mean age, overlap. The total rate continues
higher than 1.0 as long as mean age at marriage continues
to fall. A rising mean age at marriage has the opposite
effect, thinning out the occurrence of marriage until the
rise in mean age ceases. The average value of 0.885 of
the total marriage rate from 1950 to 1982 (despite the
continuation of virtually universal marriage) is the
result of the increase in mean age at marriage of about 4
years during this time. According to a formula of Norman
Ryder (1956), a period total first-marriage rate is
reduced in proportion to the average annual rate of
change of cohort age at marriage. An increase of 4 years
in 32 years should reduce the average period total
first-marriage rate by about 0.125, or to about 0.875--
very close to the actual average value of 0.885 for the
32 years in question.

MEAN AGE AT FIRST MARRIAGE

Figure 10 shows the annual value of the mean age at first
marriage from 1950 to the first half of 1982. The mean
age at first marriage calculated for the decade of the
1940s is little different from the mean for 1950 (18.46
compared with 18.68), but was a year higher than the
average (17.52) for the Chinese farm population in 1929-31
(Barclay et al., 1976). The increase in mean age was
relatively gradual in the 1950s and 1960s and relatively
rapid in the 1970s. The revolutionary government set a
legal minimum marriage age of 18 years and introduced
many changes in social organization that reduced the
incidence of very early marriage. In 1953 nearly 43
percent of women were married before reaching 18; by 1965
this fraction had fallen to about 21 percent; at the
beginning of 1982, only 4 percent had married before
reaching 18.

The mean age at marriage rose sharply after 1970: in
the 8 years from 1971 to 1979 the increase was twice what
the increase had been in the 21 years from 1950 to 1971.
The rise in age at marriage in the 1970s was certainly
enhanced, if not altogether produced, by government
pressure as part of the program to reduce the birth
rate. The official policy was later marriage, longer
birth intervals, and fewer children. Women were
encouraged to postpone marriage until age 23 in the rural
areas and until age 25 in the cities. From 1971 to 1979

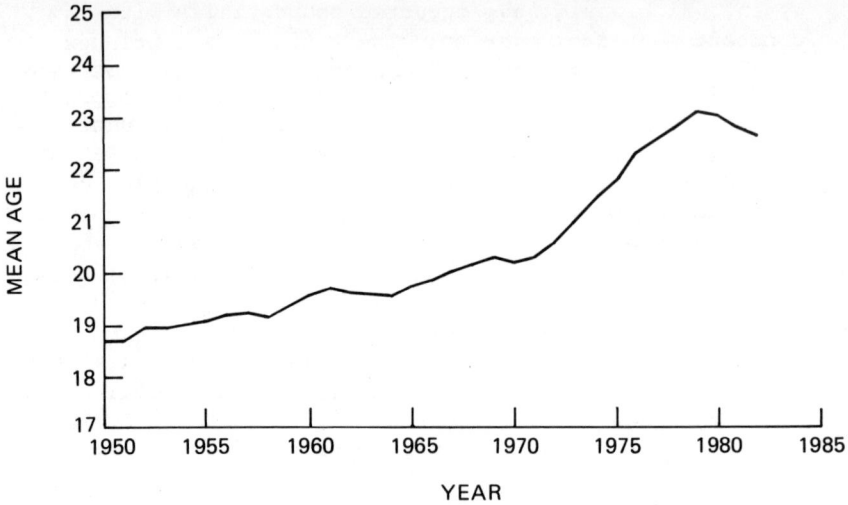

FIGURE 10 Mean Age at First Marriage of Females, 1950-82: China

the reduction in the proportion of women who had ever married before reaching age 24 was large in the rural areas and dramatic in the cities: from 89 to 76 percent in the rural population and from 68 to 20 percent in the urban population.

PATTERNS OF MARRIAGE

By cumulation of age-specific first-marriage rates, the proportion of women ever married at each age can be calculated for each cohort: that proportion is shown for selected female cohorts in Figure 11 (see Table A-4 for data for all years). From the cohort reaching age 15 in 1950 to the cohort reaching 15 in 1965, the curves showing age of attaining successively greater proportions of ever-married women moves to the right--to higher ages--with each cohort, ultimately reaching nearly 100 percent. The cohort reaching age 15 in 1970 has a relatively slow start in entering marriage, reaching 50 percent ever married at an age 2 1/2 years later than the attainment of 50 percent by the cohort only 5 years older (age 15 in 1965). However, the younger cohort made up for its slow early entry into marriage and by age 26 had

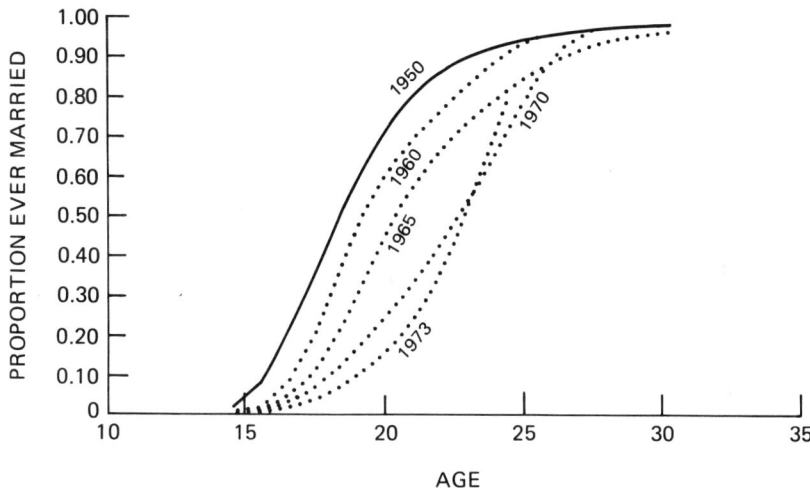

FIGURE 11 Proportion of Ever-Married Women, by Single Years of Age, Cohorts Aged 15 in 1950, 1960, 1965, 1970, and 1973: China

surpassed the proportion married that had been achieved at the same age by the older cohort. Those reaching 15 in 1973 were even slower than the 1970 cohort in entering marriage at early ages and then quickened the pace so as to surpass older cohorts—by about age 24 for the cohort 15 in 1965 and by age 23 for the cohort 15 in 1970.

In Figure 12 the curves showing cumulative entry into marriage for selected female cohorts are compared with a standard curve of cumulative first marriage. The standard curve is a mathematical function of age that with suitable choice of constants fits the marriage experience of many quite different populations. The standard distribution—an asymmetrical curve skewed to the right—fits different experiences, ranging from early-marrying to late-marrying cohorts, if the appropriate starting age (or, alternatively, the proper mean age) and the proper pace of marriage (or the proper standard deviation) is chosen. (The proportion ultimately marrying must also be specified, but in China this proportion can be estimated to a good approximation as 100 percent [Coale, 1971; Coale and McNeil, 1972]). In Figure 12, the standard curve of the proportion of ever-married women is fitted to the experience of each

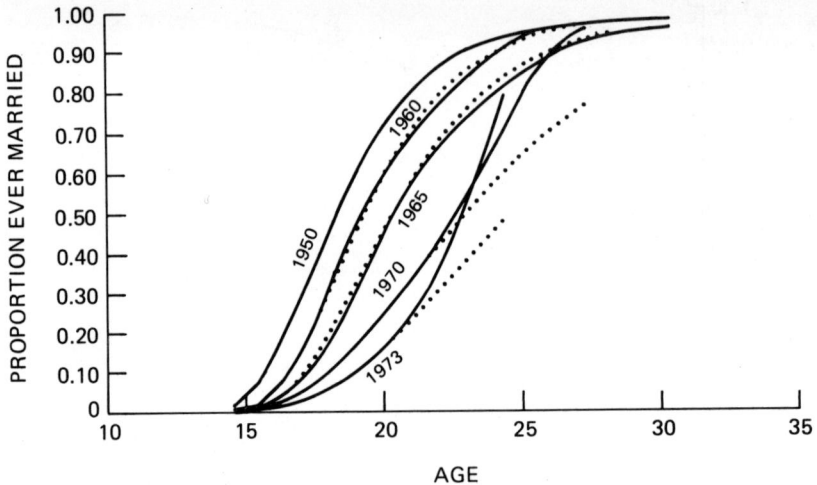

FIGURE 12 Proportion of Ever-Married Women, Cohorts Aged 15 in 1950, 1960, 1965, 1970, and 1973 (solid lines), and Standard Curves Fitted to Ages 16.5 and 20.5 (dotted lines): China

cohort by choosing two parameters (of location and spread) that forces the standard curve to pass through the cohort's recorded proportion ever married at ages 16.5 and 20.5. For cohorts reaching age 15 in 1950, 1960, and 1965, the nuptiality experience past age 20 is fitted very well indeed by the standard curves forced to pass through these early points in the cohort's entry into marriage. Those reaching 15 in 1970 also follow a standard curve fitted to the proportion ever married at 16.5 and 20.5, but only up to age 22; at higher ages the standard curve fitted to these early points rises too slowly--or, more realistically, above age 22 the cohort accelerates its entry into marriage above the slow pace it had followed up to age 22. The cohort of women aged 15 in 1973 departs still earlier and more steeply from the very slow pace of marriage it followed up to age 20.

The existence of a standard frequency distribution of first marriages has a behavioral explanation: it is generated by a normal (Gaussian) distribution of attaining an age considered as marriageable, followed by exponential distributions of the duration of three intermediate stages--the search for the ultimate spouse, the interval between finding the spouse and engagement, and between engagement and marriage (Coale and McNeil, 1972). When age at marriage is governed by accepted social norms and gradually evolving conditions, the standard distribution seems to fit very well.

In the 1970s the intensified program to reduce the birth rate included later marriage as an important component. The legal minimum of age at marriage was not increased (from the 18 years for women set in the marriage law of 1950); however, permission to marry had to be obtained from the administrative head of the work units of bride and groom, and a late marriage rate (the proportion of marriages of women older than 23 in rural areas and older than 25 in cities) was one of the aims imposed by the new population policies (Tien, 1983). Restrictions that slowed down entry into marriage for women under age 23 led to more rapid entry into marriage for women after that age: for example, see the comparison of the 15-in-1970 cohort with the fitted standard in Figure 12.

In 1980 a new marriage law was passed that increased the legal minimum marriage age for women from 18 to 20. The passage of the new law was reportedly accompanied by a relaxation of the measures that enforced later marriage because of the social problems created by postponing marriage past age 23 in a society in which women are traditionally married soon after menarche and in which sexual relations among unmarried people are not socially acceptable. The new law was accompanied by a marriage boom: the total first-marriage rate for women rose from .922 in 1979 to 1.137 in 1980, 1.303 in 1981, and 1.314 in the first half of 1982; mean age at first marriage fell from 23.1 in 1979 to 22.7 in the first half of 1982. The departure of recent cohorts from standard curves of age at marriage may be the result, then, of government action that artificially reduced rates of first marriage at early ages and led to artificially high rates at later ages, when the pressure was off. The relaxation of pressure against marriages at ages under 23 led to a marriage boom. The effects of these marriage patterns on fertility are explored in the next chapter.

CHAPTER 4

CHILDBEARING IN CHINA SINCE 1950

TOTAL FERTILITY RATES

The published report on the 1/1,000-sample survey of fertility in 1982 includes data on age-specific fertility rates by single years of age from 1950 through 1981. The published tables also include single-year rates for the rural and urban populations for these years and a separately tabulated set of rates for the total population extending back to 1940. The detailed fertility histories were obtained by interviewing women aged 15-67. Because of the upper age limit, the age-specific fertility rates presented for women aged 49 are derived from actual responses of the women interviewed only for years after 1964, rates for women aged 45 are derived from responses only after 1959, etc. The upper age limit of the women interviewed also means that all rates above age 25 in 1940 were estimated by methods not explicitly described.

As noted above, comparison of the annual number of births thus calculated with the annual number from official sources indicates that the official number of births is understated. The comparison also shows systematically lower ratios of official numbers of births to calculated numbers of births for years that have 13 lunar months. It is thus clear that the number of births reported in the fertility survey in those years was too high. Table 5 shows birth rates and total fertility rates (TFRs) based on the estimated annual number of births calculated from the fertility rates reported from the survey. Also shown in Table 5 are birth rates and TFRs adjusted for overstatement of births in years with 13 lunar months and for understatement in other years. If all births were reported by the lunar calendar, 13-month years would have 1.05 times the number of births

TABLE 5 Birth Rate and Total Fertility Rate Derived from Fertility Survey: China

Year	Unadjusted Birth Rate (per 1,000)	TFR	Adjusted[a] Birth Rate (per 1,000)	TFR
1950	46.5	5.81	41.3	5.93
1951	39.8	5.70	40.6	5.82
1952	45.1	6.47	43.7	6.26
1953	42.2	6.05	43.1	6.17
1954	43.5	6.28	44.4	6.41
1955	42.7	6.26	41.3	6.06
1956	39.4	5.85	40.2	5.97
1957	42.5	6.41	41.1	6.21
1958	36.9	5.68	37.7	5.80
1959	27.7	4.30	28.3	4.39
1960	26.0	4.02	25.2	3.89
1961	21.9	3.29	22.3	3.36
1962	40.1	6.02	40.9	6.14
1963	48.9	7.50	47.3	7.26
1964	39.9	6.18	40.7	6.31
1965	38.9	6.08	39.7	6.20
1966	39.6	6.26	38.3	6.06
1967	33.4	5.31	34.1	5.42
1968	40.4	6.45	39.1	6.24
1969	35.8	5.72	36.5	5.84
1970	36.5	5.81	37.2	5.93
1971	34.6	5.44	33.5	5.27
1972	31.8	4.98	32.4	5.08
1973	29.5	4.54	30.1	4.63
1974	28.0	4.17	27.1	4.04
1975	24.8	3.57	25.3	3.64
1976	23.2	3.24	22.5	3.14
1977	21.1	2.84	21.5	2.90
1978	20.8	2.72	21.2	2.78
1979	21.6	2.75	20.9	2.66
1980	18.1	2.24	18.5	2.29
1981	21.2	2.63	(21.2)	(2.63)
1982	21.3	2.66	(21.3)	(2.66)

[a] Adjusted to correct for effect of lunar calendar and for understatement in other years.

in a solar calendar year, and 12-month years would have .97 times the number in a solar year. The adjusted birth rates and TFRs are calculated on the assumption that two-thirds of the reported births are based on lunar years: leap-year (13-months) rates were divided by 1.033 and non-leap-year (12-months) rates by 0.98.

The unadjusted total fertility rates in Table 5 are taken directly from the report on the fertility survey, which also contains partially estimated TFRs for 1940-49, with an average value of 5.44 for that decade. This rate differs very little from the total fertility rate of 5.50 estimated by Barclay and others (1976) for the Chinese farm population in 1929-31. The total fertility rate from the survey rises to about 6.0 through the 1950s until 1958, when a dramatic decline begins. An increase in fertility from 5.5 to 6.0 as part of the first impact of modernizing forces is not unusual. It frequently occurs because of the diminished effect of various customs and practices that restrict fertility below its potential maximum in almost every less-developed country. These customs and practices, which do not vary according to the number of children already born and hence are not intended to impose a direct limit on the size of the family, include prolonged breastfeeding, periodic separation of spouses because of seasonal migration, prohibition of intercourse during lactation, etc.[7]

The most striking features of the sequence of TFRs are the dramatic reduction from 1956 to 1961 (the TFR in 1961 is only a little more than half of the TFR in 1957); the recovery in 1962 to a TFR similar to the 1950s; and the unique, very high TFR of 7.5 in 1963. The TFR in the mid-to-late 1960s was comparable to the mid-1950s except for a temporary drop in 1967, coinciding with the Cultural Revolution. A sustained decline began after 1970, reaching a low in 1980 that was more than 60 percent below the level in 1970; there was a modest recovery in 1981, but only to a fertility level still well below half the level in 1970. These episodes of a large reduction, an extraordinary recovery, and a subsequent major decline are analyzed further below.

THE EFFECT OF CHANGES IN NUPTIALITY ON THE RATE OF CHILDBEARING

Changes in age at marriage have a different effect on fertility in populations in which married couples practice little contraception and therefore have similar age-specific marital fertility rates whatever the age at marriage and in populations in which married couples effectively control fertility and attain fixed targets of completed size of family. In noncontracepting populations, increases in age at marriage reduce the number of children born to each cohort of women by reducing the number of younger women exposed to the risk of childbearing. The reduced number of younger women who are currently married causes lower fertility in each time period as well as for each cohort. In populations practicing effective contraception, changes in age at marriage alter the timing of births for each cohort of women without necessarily altering the final average size of family achieved. A postponement of childbearing caused by later marriage produces a temporary reduction in period fertility even if cohort total fertility is not changed. When age at marriage stops increasing, this temporary depression of fertility ends.

The effect of increasing age at marriage on fertility even when each cohort achieves the same family size is not generally noticed nor well understood. Imagine, for example, that all women marry at the mean age of marriage and bear only one child, one year after marriage. Suppose that for a long period the age at marriage is 22 years and that both the total first-marriage rate and the total fertility rate are 1.0. Then suppose that at a certain moment the mean age at marriage rises to 23 years. In the year following this shift, there would be no marriages because the cohort that was 22 in the preceding year would all have already married and the cohort becoming 22 in the given year would not marry until reaching 23 a year later. In the ensuing year there would be no births for a similar reason. So from a one-year increase in age at marriage (and age at childbearing) there would be a loss of a full year's quota of marriages and a full year's quota of births even though the proportion ever marrying and the completed family size for every cohort remained fixed. In a more complex change of the sort that actually occurs, a rise in the mean age at marriage within a period of time means that one year's quota of marriages is lost, not in a single year, but during a span of several years. A rise by one year in the mean age of childbearing also means the loss, over a span of years, of one year's quota of births, even though completed size of family of cohorts does not change.

The effect of changes in age at marriage on changes in the total fertility rate can be evaluated under two quite different assumptions about the fertility of the married women when age at marriage is changing. One assumption is that the fertility of married women at each age remains constant as age of entry into marriage changes. This assumption is logically tenable if there is very little contraceptive practice. The second assumption is that the fertility of married women at each duration of marriage remains fixed, with a duration-specific fertility schedule that declines quite steeply because each marriage cohort is curtailing its childbearing after the early attainment of desired family size.

The change in fertility associated with changing nuptiality in China can be estimated under both of these assumptions. First the effect of changes in age at marriage on total fertility is determined when the schedule of age-specific marital fertility is fixed. The proportion of ever-married women at each age in selected years is combined with the age-specific fertility of the ever-married women in 1956. The age pattern of marital fertility in the 1950s (see below) differs little from the age pattern characteristic of populations that do not deliberately control fertility (do not try to reduce childbearing when desired family size has been reached) by contraception or abortion. The first calculation shows the reduction in the total fertility rate that would have occurred if the virtual absence of contraception and abortion of the 1950s had continued (and if there had been no change in factors, such as duration and intensity of breastfeeding, that affect marital fertility in the absence of contraception). The data provided in the report of the 1982 fertility survey are the basis for this calculation. The proportion of ever-married women at each age in each year since 1950 is estimated by the cumulation of first-marriage rates for each cohort (see Table A-4).[8] Division of the tabulated overall age-specific fertility rate at a given age by the proportion ever married at that age yields an age-specific fertility rate of ever-married women. The next step is to multiply the proportion of ever-married women at each age in different years by the age-specific ever-married fertility rates of 1956. The results are shown in Table 6. The total fertility rate would have fallen by a little more than 20 percent from 1950 to 1980 and then risen by several percent to 1982 if the ever-married fertility rates of 1956 had been in effect. Most of the decline in

TABLE 6 Total Fertility Rate Calculated for Selected
Years, from Proportion of Women Ever Married and
Age-Specific Marital Fertility Rates, 1956: China

	Year							
	1950	1955	1960	1965	1970	1975	1980	1982
Calculated TRF	5.97	5.87	5.68	5.62	5.42	4.96	4.71	4.88
TFR of 1950=100	100	98.3	95.1	94.1	90.8	83.1	78.9	81.7

total fertility rate would have occurred after 1970, when the greater part of the rise in age at marriage occurred. The TFR in 1980 was 61 percent lower than the TFR in 1950; the decline that would have occurred from changes in marriage alone, with constant marital fertility rates, is thus about one-third of the actual decline.

The second calculation of the effects of changing nuptiality is limited to the years after 1970, when the change in nuptiality was greatest and when there was a major increase in the deliberate restriction of marital fertility by contraception and abortion. The rationale of this calculation is different from the first. Duration-specific marital fertility rates have been calculated for 1970, 1977, and 1981 from data in the 1982 fertility survey that give the number of births to women at marriage durations of 0-1, 1-2, . . ., 19-20, and 20+ years in those 3 years and from estimates of the number of ever-married women classified by duration of marriage (Song et al., 1983). The number of women by age in each year have been determined by intracohort interpolation: multiplication by the proportion ever married provides the number of ever-married women by age, and the distribution of the ever-married at each age by duration can then be ascertained from the sequence of first-marriage rates in the cohort for earlier years and younger ages. (The estimated number of ever-married women by duration of marriage from 1970 to 1982 is shown in Table A-5.) The ratio of births by duration since first marriage to number of ever-married women by duration provides a set of duration-specific ever-married fertility rates for 1970, 1977, and 1981 (see Table A-6). The next step is to assume that the married women in each year from 1970 on were subject to 1981 duration-

specific fertility rates. This assumption is based on
the hypothesis that women during the 1970s were as
effective in limiting marital fertility at every stage of
marriage as were women at the corresponding stage of
marriage in 1981. Such a hypothesis is acceptable (even
as an hypothesis) only when it incorporates a schedule of
duration-specific fertility that falls off rapidly after
relatively high values at early durations, because only
then would it be possible for duration-specific fertility
to remain unchanged when mean age at marriage increases.
When fertility is little controlled (as in 1956) women
marrying at age 25 might have about the same fertility at
each duration during the first 10 years of marriage as
women marrying at 21, but not in the 20th year, when
reduced capacity for reproduction would cause lower
fertility among those who had married at 25.

In short, the calculation of the births that would
have occurred from 1970 to 1981 with the duration-
specific fertility rates of 1981 illustrates the change
in total fertility rate that would have resulted from
changes in age at marriage, even if each cohort had
maintained lifetime fertility approximately constant but
had shifted the time of childbearing by marrying later.
Table 7 shows the results. There were almost 30 million
births in 1970; with 1981 duration-specific fertility
there would have been only about 16 million. The TFR in
1970 would have been only 3.09 with 1981 duration-
specific rates; it was 5.81. Had the rates remained
unchanged at the low level, the TFR would have declined
from 3.09 in 1970 to a low of 2.41 in 1979 and then risen
to 2.85 in 1981. With no change in duration-specific
fertility rates (and therefore approximately constant
cohort total fertility), there would have been a decline
to only 78 percent of the 1970 TFR in 1979 and then a
recovery to 92 percent in 1982.

The two calculations--with constant age-specific
fertility rates (as of 1956) and constant duration-
specific rates (as of 1981)--illustrate different sorts
of influence that changes in age at marriage can have on
overall fertility. The first calculation shows that had
there been no increased use of contraception (and no
change in "natural" fertility from reduced breastfeeding),
the TFR would have fallen by about 20 percent from 1950
to 1980 because rising age at marriage would have reduced
the average exposure to married life and the attendant
risk of childbearing. The second calculation shows that
even with fixed, highly controlled marital fertility in

TABLE 7 Annual Births (in millions), Total Fertility Rate, 1970-82: China

Year	Actual Number of Births (in millions)	Births with 1981 Duration-Specific Fertility (in millions)	Actual Total Fertility Rate (per 1,000 women)	Total Fertility Rate with 1981 Duration-Specific Fertility (per 1,000 women)
1970	29.84	15.87	5.81	3.09
1971	28.94	16.30	5.44	3.06
1972	27.38	16.32	4.98	2.97
1973	26.05	16.30	4.54	2.84
1974	25.18	16.31	4.17	2.70
1975	22.64	16.41	3.57	2.59
1976	21.58	16.69	3.24	2.50
1977	19.93	17.15	2.84	2.44
1978	19.93	17.67	2.72	2.41
1979	20.93	18.32	2.75	2.41
1980	17.73	19.39	2.24	2.45
1981	21.03	21.03	2.63	2.63
1982	21.56[a]	23.13	2.66[a]	2.85

Note: Actual numbers and rates; hypothetical numbers and rates resulting from duration-specific fertility of 1981.

[a]Estimated.

which childbearing beyond the early durations of marriage is severely limited, the TFR would have declined by about 20 percent from 1970 to 1979 because rising age at marriage during these years would have reduced the number of married women at early durations. Recall that the total first-marriage rate was low during most of the 1970s (as low as 0.64) despite the continuation of universal entry into marriage cohort by cohort. The increase in mean age at marriage that was the principal source of low total marriage rates also produced a reduced number of women in the early durations of marriage. The cessation and slight reversal of the increase in age at marriage, plus the marriage boom associated with the new marriage law of 1980, produced a phenomenal increase in the total marriage rate and a commensurate increase in the number of marriages of short duration. A consequence is that a rise in overall fertility by 18 percent (from a TFR of 2.41 in 1979 to one of 2.85 in 1982) would have occurred with constant fertility by duration of marriage.

The report of the 1982 fertility survey does not provide a time series of age-specific rates of fertility by order of birth, but it does show such rates for 1980 and 1981. The total first-birth rate (the sum over all childbearing ages of age-specific rates of bearing a first child) rose from 0.869 in 1980 to 1.162 in 1981—nearly three-fourths of the increase in the total fertility rate. (Of the increase in the TFR, 90 percent is in the total first-birth rate plus the total second-birth rate, both increases largely the result of compression in 1981 of first and second births by women at different ages into the same time period because of the marriage boom and the reduction in age at marriage.) Some increase in fertility would occur with constant duration-specific fertility even if age at marriage merely stopped rising. If the continued increase in age at marriage had ceased and not reversed, the total first- marriage rate would have returned to about 1.0; the persistent shortage in the annual number of first marriages caused by rising mean age at marriage would have ended.

AGE PATTERNS OF MARITAL FERTILITY

One of the benefits of the detailed information that appears in the report of the 1982 fertility survey is the feasibility of calculating age-specific marital fertility schedules. To do so, the proportion of ever-married women by age is determined from the data on first marriages; a fertility schedule of the ever-married women is then obtained by dividing the overall fertility of women at each age by the proportion ever married. Finally, the marital fertility schedule is derived by a further division of the ever-married rate at each age by the estimated proportion of currently married to ever-married women. This last proportion can be estimated as having approximately the same values in different calendar years because of the surprisingly little difference between it in 1982 and in the Chinese farm population in 1930. The proprortion of currently married to ever-married women at the two dates are as follows:

	Age				
Year	20-24	25-29	30-34	35-39	40-44
1982	.986	.977	.960	.933	.888
1929-31	.981	.968	.953	.916	.860

The very slight difference in these ratios despite the very substantial difference in mortality implies that the higher incidence of widowhood at the earlier date must have been offset by a high rate of remarriage of widows. Approximate age-specific marital fertility schedules by single years of age from 20 through 39 have been calculated for selected years. In every year the ratio of currently married to ever-married women was assumed equal to the average of the ratios for 1929-31 and 1982.

In Figure 13, marital fertility rates are shown relative to a schedule of "natural" fertility, with the ratio to natural fertility at ages 20-24 set equal to 1.00. The comparison with natural fertility provides indirect evidence of the extent to which marital fertility is affected by deliberate control through the use of contraception and abortion. Louis Henry (1961) was the first to note that the age pattern of marital fertility was similar in different populations in which couples do not practice contraception or take other measures to reduce fertility after a certain family size is reached; he called such fertility "natural." In

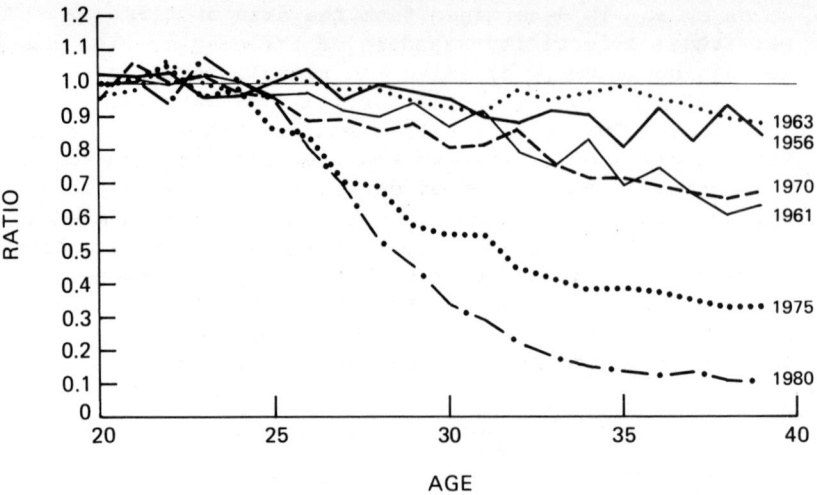

FIGURE 13 Ratio of Age-Specific Marital Fertility to Natural Fertility (with ratio at 20-24 set at 1.00), 1956, 1961, 1970, 1975, and 1980: China

Figure 13, the calculated marital fertility rates are divided by a set of natural fertility rates, with the two schedules--a schedule for China and an average of natural fertility schedules selected for good quality of data from those cited by Henry (Coale and Trussell, 1974)--brought to the same average at ages 20-24. In 1956 the ratio of marital fertility to natural fertility remains above 0.9 except for two points that are probably the result of sampling variation or slightly inexact reporting by respondents who were over age 60 in 1982. In 1961 the TFR was only 56 percent of the TFR in 1956; the reduction in marital fertility was large at younger ages (a 34 percent reduction at 20-24) as well as at older ages (a 49 percent reduction at 35-39). To achieve the modestly increased departure as age increases from the low level of natural fertility schedule in 1961 would entail only a modest use of deliberate limitation by older women.

Low fertility among young as well as older married women in 1961 is consistent with restriction of child-bearing caused not only by contraception but by social disruption and the famine conditions in 1960. As noted below, a very high peak in the death rate occurred in 1960, the result of a famine associated with crop failures induced by a combination of chaotic economic conditions, drought, and floods. Famine is known to prevent ovulation and to reduce male libido. Disruption of normal family life while the population was mobilized for various projects and engaged in searches for food, like the direct effects of famine on reproductive capacity, would cause fertility to fall at all ages. The death-rate peak in 1960 implies that 1960 was the worst of the crisis; reduced conceptions in 1960 would produce a very low TFR in 1961. The slightly steeper reduction in marital fertility relative to natural fertility as age increases in 1961 compared with 1956 may have been caused by the greater susceptability of older women to fertility impairment during a famine. A further indication of a quasi-biological basis for the very low marital fertility in 1961 is the height of the peak in fertility reached in 1963. The TFR of 7.50 in 1963 is well above the highest TFR during the 1950s (6.41 in 1957). The age structure of marital fertility in 1963 is very similar to 1956, but at a much higher level. The 1963/1956 ratio of marital fertility rates by five-year intervals for women aged 20-24 to 35-39 varies only from 1.33 to 1.38. The 1963/1961 ratio of marital fertility rates increases from 2.06 at 20-24 to 2.70 at 35-39, possibly because of the cessation of whatever slight degree of contraceptive practice there may have been in 1960-61 or possibly because the catastrophic situation in 1960-61 impaired the fertility of older women more than the fertility of younger women. Marital fertility that is at least one-third higher in 1963 than in 1956 at every five-year age interval from 20 to 40 implies a much higher than normal susceptability to pregnancy. The source of such above-normal susceptability was doubtless an abnormally low proportion of women who had recently given birth (who experience many months without ovulation if they breastfeed) and also an abnormally high number of newlyweds (the total first-marriage rate in 1962 was 1.19).

In sum, the very low fertility of 1961 was probably caused by the disruption of normal married life and by famine-induced subfecundity; the unequaled high fertility of 1963 resulted from the restoration of normal marital life, from an abnormally large number of marriages, and from the unusually small fraction of married women who were infertile because of nursing a recently born infant. The age structure of marital fertility was essentially that of natural fertility, unaffected by

deliberate restriction, in 1956 and again in 1963. At
the low point in 1961, marital fertility fell with age
slightly more steeply than does natural fertility. This
pattern may have resulted either from some practice of
folk methods of contraception or abortion or from a
greater biological effect of the crisis on older women.
In 1970 the decline of marital fertility with age
relative to natural fertility closely paralleled the
corresponding curve for 1961 (see Figure 13 above); but
in 1970 this decline was almost certainly the result of
an increase in deliberate control with age and not to the
biological factors that may have affected older women
disproportionately in 1960-61. In 1975 the steep fall of
fertility relative to natural fertility clearly shows the
much greater effect of fertility restriction among older
women; by 1980 the decline in marital fertility with age
is comparable to the structure of marital fertility in
highly developed societies with total fertility rates
below replacement levels.

DIFFERENTIAL FERTILITY

Urban/Rural Differences

The 1982 sample fertility survey provides annual data on
fertility and nuptiality in the detail already described
for the rural and urban populations as well as for the
total. The TFRs for the rural and urban populations are
given in Table 8 and shown graphically in Figure 14. In
the early 1950s average overall urban fertility increased
relative to rural fertility from about 80 to about 90
percent, and it remained at a constant ratio of about 90
percent until 1959 and 1960; evidently, rural fertility
was more affected by the Great Leap Forward than was
urban fertility. From 1960 to 1966 the ratio of rural to
urban TFR fell to about 50 percent, and since then the
ratio has been nearly constant. In absolute terms, rural
fertility in 1964 returned (after the crisis deficit and
the postcrisis peak) to about the level of the 1950s,
while urban fertility barely surpassed its 1957 level
even in 1963, fell steeply for a few years after 1963,
recovered somewhat in 1968, and then fell at the same
relative rate as did rural fertility. The decline of
urban fertility from 90 percent of rural fertility in the
late 1950s to about 50 percent in the late 1960s (while
rural fertility remained little changed) appears to

TABLE 8 Total Fertility Rates, Rural and Urban Populations, 1950-81: China

Year	Total Fertility Rate		
	Rural	Urban	Urban/Rural
1950	5.963	5.001	.839
1951	5.904	4.719	.799
1952	6.667	5.521	.828
1953	6.183	5.402	.874
1954	6.390	5.732	.897
1955	6.391	5.665	.886
1956	5.974	5.333	.893
1957	6.504	5.943	.914
1958	5.775	5.253	.910
1959	4.323	4.172	.965
1960	3.996	4.057	1.015
1961	3.349	2.982	.890
1962	6.303	4.789	.760
1963	7.784	6.207	.797
1964	6.567	4.395	.669
1965	6.597	3.749	.568
1966	6.958	3.104	.446
1967	5.847	2.905	.497
1968	7.025	3.872	.551
1969	6.263	3.299	.527
1970	6.379	3.267	.512
1971	6.011	2.882	.479
1972	5.503	2.637	.479
1973	5.008	2.387	.477
1974	4.642	1.982	.427
1975	3.951	1.782	.451
1976	3.582	1.608	.449
1977	3.116	1.574	.505
1978	2.968	1.551	.523
1979	3.045	1.373	.451
1980	2.480	1.147	.463
1981	2.910	1.390	.478

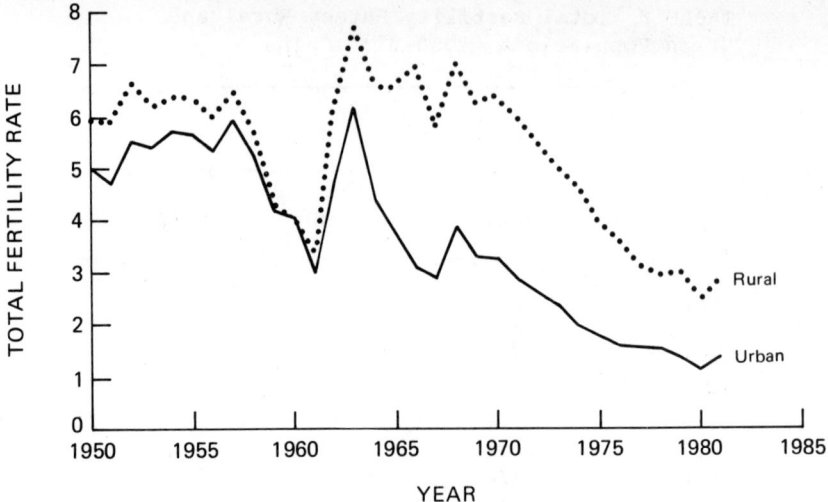

FIGURE 14 Total Fertility Rates, Rural and Urban Populations, 1950-81: China

conform to the classic picture often ascribed to (but not always followed by) European fertility during the so-called demographic transition: the urban population has a higher age at marriage; it starts deliberate family limitation before the rural population does; and after the transition starts in the rural population, the urban population continues to have lower rates of childbearing. The early timing of the urban decline has a simpler explanation, however: the antinatalist program was initiated earlier and pursued more vigorously in the cities.

Age-specific fertility rates of the rural and urban populations in 1955, 1968, and 1980 are compared in Figure 15. In 1955 the difference between rural and urban TFRs is composed almost equally of lower fertility below age 25 in the cities (caused by later marriage) and lower fertility above age 31 in the cities (caused by a modest prevalence of contraception and abortion or possibly by a higher proportion of widows). In 1968, the rural fertility schedule looks much like the schedule in 1955 though slightly higher, except at the younger ages, where slightly later marriage reduced fertility. The early part of the urban schedule in 1968 shows the strong effect of later marriage and the later part the strong

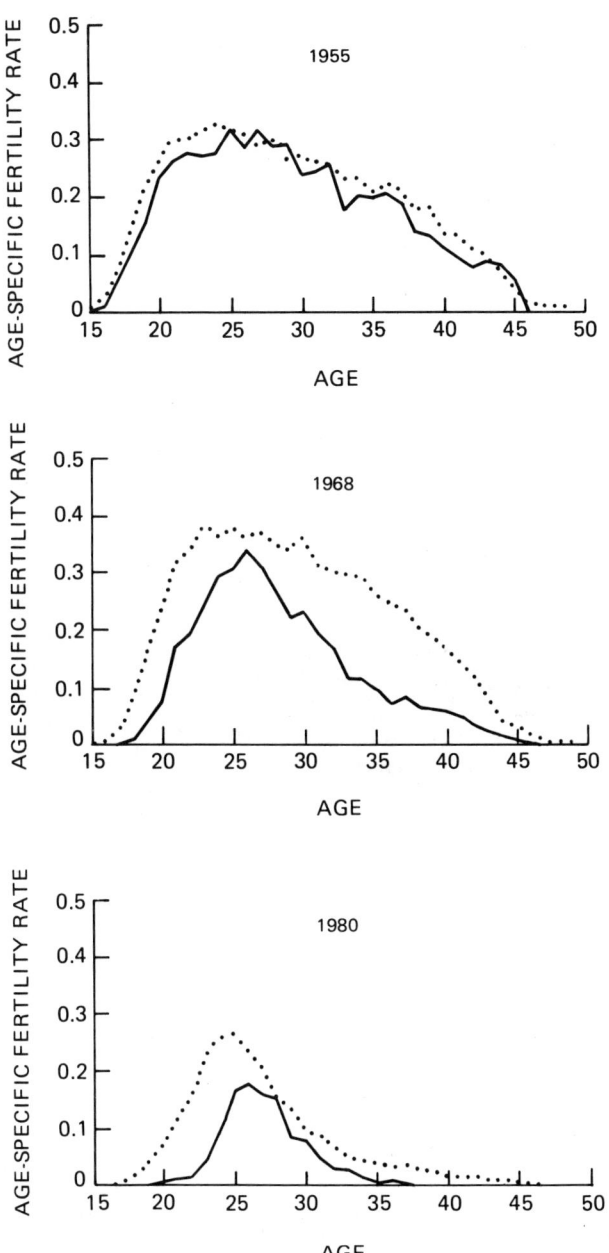

FIGURE 15 Age-Specific Fertility Rates, Rural (dotted line) and Urban (solid line) Populations, 1955, 1968, and 1980: China

effect of deliberate birth control. By 1980 these
effects are evident in the rural fertility schedule but
are still stronger for the urban schedule.

Han and Minority Group Differences

Another major difference in fertility in China is
revealed by data on the childbearing rates of the rural
Han population (the dominant Chinese ethnic group) and
those of the ethnic minorities, with a total population
of some 60 million persons (6 percent of the population).
(Li et al., 1983). The minorities have been exempt from
most of the pressures of the official antinatalist
program, are generally more isolated and less educated,
have strong pronatalist traditions, and have much higher
fertility. In 1981 the TFR of the minority populations
was 5.05 compared with 2.76 for the rural Han. The
age-specific fertility schedule of the minorities shows
the effect of earlier marriage up to age 25 and less
effective control of fertility at higher ages (Figure 16).

Other Fertility Determinants

There are also differences in fertility for women with
different levels of education and with differences in
occupation. In 1982 the average number of children ever
born to women aged 35-49 was 4.74 for illiterate women,
3.81 for women with primary school education, 3.08 for
women finishing junior high school, 2.41 for women
finishing senior high school, and 1.94 for university-
educated women. (These figures, taken from the report of
the survey, are subject to the following bias: the women
at higher levels of education are more concentrated near
age 35 in the 35-49 age interval because of rapid change
in education in China; their average parity is lowered by
this compositional feature.) At age 50 farmers had an
average parity of 5.95, workers of 4.27, and cadres of
3.10 (Li and Zhang, 1983; Zhao and Sun, 1983).

CONTRACEPTIVE PRACTICE IN CHINA

In a chapter entitled "Birth Control of Women of
Reproductive Age" in the special issue of *Population and
Economics* (Qui et al., 1983) devoted to the large-scale

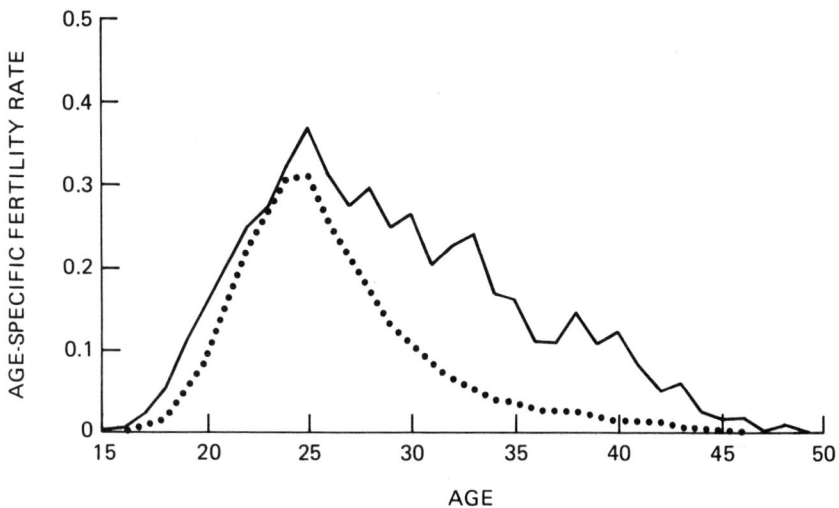

FIGURE 16 Age-Specific Fertility Rates, Ethnic Minority Women (solid line) and Rural Han Women (dotted line), 1981: China

fertility survey, it is reported that 69.5 percent of married women aged 15-49 were practicing contraception in 1982. Of these, 25 percent used female sterilization, 10 percent male sterilization, 50 percent IUDs, 8 percent the pill, and 6 percent condom and other (Qui et al., 1983). The overall rate of use is not very different from Taiwan (65 percent), Hong Kong (72 percent), or Japan (69 percent), but the use of sterilization was more frequent in China than in those neighboring populations (Population Reference Bureau, 1983).

CHAPTER 5

MORTALITY IN CHINA

METHODS

The accuracy of age reporting and the apparent consistency of coverage in the censuses of 1953, 1964, and 1982 makes it possible to construct life tables for each intercensal period, life tables that express the average mortality during the intervals of 1953-64 and 1964-82. Calculation of life tables expressing survival rates and death rates beginning at age zero is possible because the accurate age-specific fertility rates reported from the fertility survey provide the basis for accurate determination of the number of births for each intercensal year.

The construction of life tables is facilitated by a set of relations that are exactly fulfilled in any population that does not gain or lose by migration. The relation relevant to the construction of an intercensal life table is

$$N(x) = N(0) e^{-\int_0^x r(y) dy} (\ell_x/\ell_0) ,$$

where $N(x)$ is the total number of persons who attain exact age x during a specified time period, $r(y)$ is the average rate of increase of persons at age y during the period, and ℓ_x/ℓ_0 is the proportion of persons surviving from birth to age x in a hypothetical cohort subject at each age to the mean death rate at that age in the intercensal period. The mean death rate is defined as the total number of deaths in a given age interval during the time period divided by the total number of person-years-lived in that age interval. This equation can be solved for ℓ_x/ℓ_0, i.e.,

$$\ell_x/\ell_0 = (N(x)/N(0))e^{\int_0^X r(y)dy} .$$

Consequently, to construct a life table it is necessary only to estimate the total number who attain each single year of age x during the intercensal period and to calculate the average growth rates ($_1r_0$, $_1r_1$, $_1r_2$, etc.) of persons at age zero to 1, 1 to 2, etc. during the period. To be precise, these rates are the increase in the number of persons at a given age (say 10-11) divided by the number of person-years-lived at that age. If $N(x)$ is the number attaining age x, the number of person-years-lived from x to x + 1 is approximately $(N(x) + N(x+1))/2$.

In short, a highly precise life table can be formulated for the period between two censuses if the number attaining each age $N(x)$ can be determined with precision. If the census age distributions recorded in the two censuses are exact and the annual number of births is accurately recorded, $N(x)$ can be accurately calculated. The technique for accurate determination of $N(x)$ is cohort interpolation. For example, it is possible to estimate the number of people who attained exact age 10 of those who were 6-7 in 1953 and 17-18 in 1964 by subtracting a fraction of the total decrease in this cohort during those 11 years. The overall decrease is the number of deaths the cohort experienced between ages 6-7 and ages 17-18; the relevant fraction of the decrease is the proportion of deaths from 6.5 to 17.5 that occur between 6.5 and 10.0. This fraction--an interpolation factor--can be taken roughly as 3.5/11 (on the assumption of an even distribution of deaths) or, more precisely, from a model life table at an approximately appropriate level of mortality.[9]

When the number of people attaining age x has been determined for each cohort that passes through x between the censuses, $N(x)$ is found by taking the total for all such cohorts. The number at age zero is the number of births between the censuses, which is equal to the sum of the number of births calculated for each intercensal year from the number of women at each age from 15 to 49 multiplied by the age-specific fertility rates. Annual births are divided into male and female on the assumption of 106 male births for every 100 female births (51.5 percent male).

LIFE TABLES

The female life tables are more soundly based than the male life tables, because it was necessary to correct the number of males at young adult ages (see above). Abridged life tables for each sex are given in Table 9.

Expectation of life at birth (the mean duration of life or average age at death) according to the average mortality in 1953-64 was 42.2 years for males and 45.6 years for females. In 1964-82 it rose to 61.6 years for males and 63.2 for females. An increase of nearly 20 years in life expectancy in about 15 years is a very rapid increase indeed, even when allowance is made for the high mortality in 1959-61.

Two other data sources from which life tables for China can be calculated were noted earlier, the 1973-75 epidemiological survey and a large-scale survey in 1978. Figure 17 shows female mortality rates at ages 0-1, 1-5, 5-10, 10-15, . . . 80-85 for the two intercensal life tables and the two survey-based sources. The age pattern of mortality is quite similar, and the evolution of mortality rates is in the expected direction. Since the sample data from the 1978 survey were inflated to match exactly the official year-end population and the official figure for the number of deaths, it follows that the death rates derived from the survey are, on average, a little too low.

The 1982 census collected information about deaths in 1981, classified by age and sex, in each household. A life table calculated on the basis of those reported deaths and the 1981 age distribution derived from the 1982 census was presented in March 1984 at the international seminar on the 1982 census held in Beijing (Jiang et al., 1984). According to this life table, there was a further increase in expectation of life at birth to 66.4 years for males and 69.4 years for females.

CRUDE DEATH RATES

The crude death rate from 1953 to 1982 based on the officially recorded number of deaths is shown in Table 10 together with an estimated sequence in which the rates are adjusted for underreporting. The adjustment for each year is based on a crude estimate of the annual proportion underreported, an estimate based on the assumption of rising completeness of recorded deaths until 1964 and

TABLE 9 Abridged Life Tables, Male and Female, 1953-64 and 1964-82: China

	Male			Female		
Age	l(x)	m(x)	e(x)	l(x)	m(x)	e(x)
1953-64						
0	1.00000	0.13789	42.20	1.00000	0.14212	45.58
1	0.87101	0.02354	47.38	0.86731	0.02586	51.47
5	0.79368	0.00630	47.85	0.78315	0.00708	52.85
10	0.76909	0.00384	44.31	0.75592	0.00360	49.67
15	0.75443	0.00498	40.11	0.74243	0.00314	45.52
20	0.73588	0.00680	36.05	0.73087	0.00433	41.20
25	0.71127	0.00849	32.21	0.71521	0.00618	37.04
30	0.68168	0.01010	28.50	0.69344	0.00728	33.12
35	0.64807	0.01415	24.84	0.66863	0.01024	29.26
40	0.60372	0.01880	21.48	0.63521	0.01332	25.66
45	0.54948	0.02373	18.35	0.59427	0.01560	22.25
50	0.48786	0.03133	15.34	0.54964	0.01894	18.86
55	0.41688	0.04424	12.52	0.49989	0.02660	15.48
60	0.33366	0.06446	10.00	0.43737	0.04169	12.32
65	0.24090	0.09186	7.88	0.35446	0.06450	9.59
70	0.15125	0.13100	6.10	0.25580	0.09824	7.31
75	0.07754	0.18663	4.63	0.15518	0.14834	5.44
80	0.02968	0.26500	3.47	0.07246	0.22303	3.96
85	0.00747	0.37475	2.56	0.02271	0.33336	2.82
90+	0.00103	0.53677	1.86	0.00388	0.50614	1.98
1964-82						
0	1.00000	0.05042	61.64	1.00000	0.05467	63.22
1	0.95082	0.00616	63.81	0.94679	0.00700	65.75
5	0.92778	0.00292	61.36	0.92078	0.00334	63.57
10	0.91437	0.00122	57.24	0.90555	0.00120	59.61
15	0.90882	0.00190	52.57	0.90014	0.00167	54.95
20	0.90022	0.00308	48.04	0.89267	0.00229	50.39
25	0.88648	0.00338	43.75	0.88249	0.00267	45.94
30	0.87162	0.00357	39.45	0.87077	0.00315	41.52
35	0.85618	0.00381	35.12	0.85718	0.00374	37.14
40	0.84002	0.00442	30.74	0.84131	0.00435	32.80
45	0.82165	0.00618	26.37	0.82322	0.00572	28.46
50	0.79664	0.01025	22.12	0.79999	0.00864	24.21
55	0.75676	0.01681	18.14	0.76611	0.01319	20.16
60	0.69556	0.02793	14.51	0.71711	0.02165	16.36
65	0.60441	0.04507	11.29	0.64322	0.03542	12.93
70	0.48150	0.07363	8.51	0.53813	0.05755	9.95
75	0.33133	0.11940	6.22	0.40223	0.09216	7.44
80	0.17967	0.19251	4.39	0.25155	0.14698	5.39
85	0.06596	0.30775	3.01	0.11799	0.23294	3.79
90+	0.01279	0.49929	2.00	0.03480	0.38571	2.59

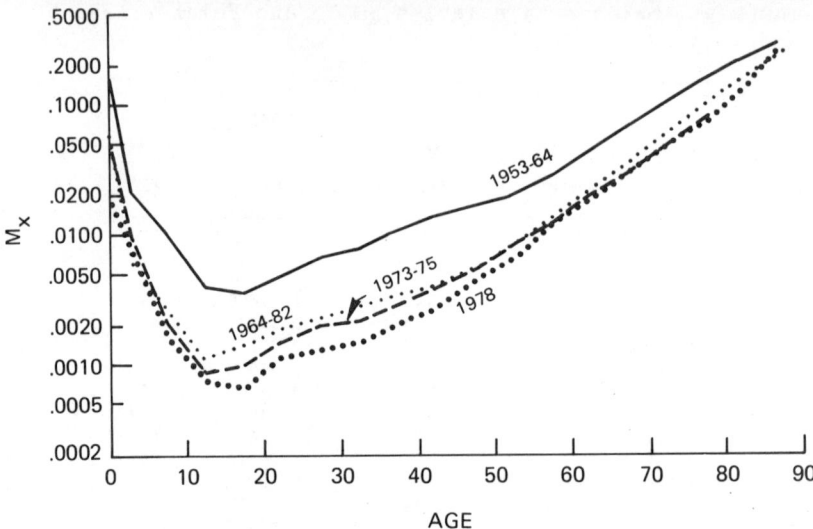

FIGURE 17 Age-Specific Mortality Rates, Females, 1953-64, 1964-82, 1973-75, and 1978: China

constant thereafter. The officially recorded deaths show a large reduction in the crude death rate, interrupted by an increase during the crisis years of 1958-61, with a peak rate of over 25 deaths per 1,000 population in 1960.

Because deaths were much less completely recorded in 1953-64 than in 1964-82, it is clear that the true decline in the death rate was much greater than indicated by the official rates. The crisis years of greatly elevated mortality are within the first intercensal period, when in 11 years an estimated 38 percent of deaths were not recorded, but completeness of recording probably improved and the crisis was near the end of the intercensal interval. In the next interval from 1964 to 1982 only 16 percent of deaths were not recorded. The adjusted deaths given in Table 10 are based on the assumption that about 55 percent of deaths were recorded from 1953 to 1956 and that completeness of recording then rose to 84 percent in 1964, with an average completeness of 62 percent. On this assumption, about 66 percent of deaths were reported in 1960, implying a crude death rate of nearly 39 per 1,000. The number of deaths calculated from the officially listed death rate is 5.90 million in

TABLE 10 Crude Death Rates (per 1,000), 1953-81: China

Year	From Official Sources	Roughly Corrected for Understatement
1953	14.0	25.5
1954	13.18	29.1
1955	12.28	22.4
1956	11.40	20.8
1957	10.80	19.0
1958	11.98	20.4
1959	14.59	23.3
1960	25.43	38.8
1961	14.24	20.5
1962	10.02	13.7
1963	10.04	13.0
1964	11.50	13.5
1965	9.50	11.1
1966	8.83	10.4
1967	8.43	9.9
1968	8.21	9.6
1969	8.03	9.4
1970	7.60	8.9
1971	7.32	8.6
1972	7.61	8.9
1973	7.04	8.3
1974	7.34	8.6
1975	7.32	8.6
1976	7.25	8.5
1977	6.87	8.1
1978	6.25	7.3
1979	6.21	7.3
1980	6.20	7.3
1981	6.19	7.3

1957 and 8.02 million in 1964. Had deaths followed a linear trend from 5.9 million to 8.0 million over these years, the total number of deaths in 1958-63 would have been 41.8 million. The number derived from officially recorded death rates is 57.4 million; by this calculation the crisis led to an excess of about 16 million deaths. The number of deaths in 1957 and 1964 adjusted for underregistration are 10.4 and 9.4 million. With a linear trend, the adjusted total number of deaths in 1958-63 would have been 59.4 million. The actual total (adjusted for estimated underregis- tration) is 86.2 million, an excess above the linear trend of about 27 million deaths. Thus, excess deaths are 16 million with no allowance for underreporting and 27 million with a rough allowance.

VARIATION OVER TIME

A comparison of the number of persons enumerated at each single year of age in 1982 (from 0-1 to 30-31) with the constructed number of births in each year from 1952 to 1982 provides partial additional evidence of the time variation of mortality in China. If the number of births from July 1 to June 30 were known exactly and if the census enumeration had been exact, the ratio of the enumerated population at age x to x + 1 to the number of births from July 1 x years before 1982 to June 30 x + 1 years before 1982 would be a cohort survival rate. (See note 4 for a description of how fiscal year births were estimated.) The sequence of cohort survival rates indicates which cohorts suffered heavy mortality and which suffered relatively light mortality. These survival rates are shown in Table 3 (above), as are the number of births estimated for each fiscal year and the number in the corresponding cohort in 1982. The survival rate is 0.9 or higher for cohorts born in 1968-69 or later, is at its lowest for cohorts born in 1966-67 and 1963-64, and is below 0.8 for all cohorts born before 1961-62 except 1959-60.

These calculated cohort survival rates do not support the natural hypothesis of especially high infant and child mortality in the cohorts born during the crisis years. The survival rate for the birth cohort of 1960-61 is lower than the survival rate of adjacent cohorts, but not as low as the survival rate of the cohorts born in 1958-59 and earlier. The implied proportions surviving to age 5 in these cohorts, given the proportion surviving from 1964 to 1982, are no higher than 75 to 80 percent.

CHAPTER 6

CONCLUSIONS

The welcome flood of accurate demographic data from China provides an unusually detailed depiction of an extraordinary population. Being the most populous nation in the world has not prevented the People's Republic of China from compressing into a short time very big reductions in fertility (more than 50 percent in a decade) and mortality (more than 20 years added to the expectation of life at birth in about 15 years). The earliest data are not inconsistent with the fertility (about the same TFR) and nuptiality (marriage about 1 year later) of traditional China, as reconstructed from a survey around 1930. The latest data are not inconsistent with some of the principal demographic characteristics of developed countries two or three decades ago. The most recent TFR in China is about the same as in the United States or a typical population in Western Europe in the 1960s; the recent average duration of life is not far from that attained in those populations about 30 years ago. Age at marriage has also changed from the very early norms traditional in much of Asia to ages more like those found in the West.

The rapid changes of fertility, mortality, and nuptiality in China have not been without costs (the excess mortality and abnormal reduction with subsequent abnormal recovery in fertility in the "bitter years"). That the surprisingly rapid changes have also incurred grave social costs can be inferred from the recent decision to reduce pressure for late marriage and from the anomalous high male/female ratio of births of second and higher order in 1981. The marriage boom of 1981-82 is not the only obstacle to attaining and maintaining very low fertility. Further upward pressure on the birth rate in the late 1980s is built into the age distribution of

China's population. In contrast to the reduced number of women in their early 20s in 1982 (because of the greatly reduced birth cohorts for 1958-61), during the next few years the much larger birth cohorts of 1963-70 will be in the normal ages of first marriage and soon thereafter in the very fertile years following marriage.

Doubtless there will be surprises, setbacks, and severe social costs among the future developments in the population of China. The changes will be better understood and the basis for policy sounder if the authorities continue to monitor the dynamics of the Chinese population closely and to continue to publish the data they collect. However, a rich lode of useful information is still to be extracted from the censuses and the fertility survey. This report has used only a fraction of the published data from the survey and has hardly touched the information contained in the census. Analysis of the sort attempted here can be extended to a separate treatment of mortality by sex and to the demography of various subgroups--the population of provinces, persons of various social and economic characteristics, etc. Continued analysis of the data already collected will be as valuable as the continued compilation of new data.

NOTES

1. The analyses based on the sample assumes that the survivors, i.e., those in the sample, do not differ in their fertility experience from nonsurvivors. There is much evidence that this assumption is true and that if there are any differences, they are trivial and do not affect the analyses.
2. The life tables are constructed by an extension of a method devised by Preston and Coale (1982). In brief, the construction involves calculating the number of persons who cross each exact age x in the intercensal period, an estimate derived by interpolation between the number enumerated in each cohort in the earlier and later censuses. When the data are accurate, the method yields a life table that is an exact expression of intercensal mortality by age. A full description of the method is contained in Coale (1984).
3. A more precise estimate can be obtained for each single year of age by allowing for the fact that the proportion surviving from one age to another is not an exactly linear sequence. More appropriate, slightly nonlinear interpolation is achieved by deriving interpolation factors from a model life table at about the right level of mortality.
4. The births derived from the age-specific fertility rates are for calendar years (January 1 to December 31); the births compatible with the census age distributions are for "fiscal" years (July 1 to June 30) because the censuses were taken as of midyear. Fiscal-year births were estimated by a division of the calendar year births into first-half-year and second-half-year births. The difference between first-half-year and second-half-year births was taken

as one-fourth the difference between the births in the preceding year and in the following year. These half-year births were then recombined on a fiscal year basis.
5. It should be noted that a "stopping rule"--no more births after a boy is born, but possibly another after the birth of a girl--is well known <u>not</u> to increase the male/female ratio.
6. The age-specific rates for 1981-82 were obtained by assuming the continuation to the first half of 1982 of the 1981 rates.
7. It is also possible that older women understate the number of births that occurred to them a long time ago and that such understatement may contribute to the low estimates of fertility in the 1940s from this survey. However, the rates are in agreement with data about Chinese farmers, and the agreement of the numbers projected from the births in the 1950s to the 1982 census with the single-year distribution in that census is a convincing indication of no substantial understatement of the births reported as occurring nearly 30 years before the survey.
8. For cohorts that began entering marriage before 1950, the proportion ever married at each age was determined by subtracting first-marriage rates from 0.999, assigned to the age above which no more first marriages in the cohort were reported.
9. This method of life table construction is fully described in an article by Ansley Coale (1984). Constructed examples with artificially perfect data show that the life table is exact if the data used are exact.

APPENDIX: DATA TABLES

TABLE A-1 Calculated Number of Women by Single Years of Age, Aged 15-49 for Each Year, Estimated by Cohort Interpolation (in 100s), 1953-82: China

	1953	1954	1955	1956	1957	1958	1959	1960	1961	1962	1963	1964	1965	1966	1967
15	46697	47411	47988	50748	52425	49695	51587	53509	59019	62470	62466	64154	73837	73341	85660
16	47587	46763	47383	47854	50500	52249	49498	51430	53450	58868	62129	62033	63662	73793	73238
17	49647	47586	46835	47353	47712	50235	52144	51261	52806	53386	53318	61764	61517	63625	73745
18	55327	49551	47584	46912	47320	47557	49948	51986	49060	51079	53318	58531	61230	61436	63583
19	50876	54656	49448	47582	46994	47285	47393	49642	51819	48817	50886	53245	57932	61128	61349
20	49963	50619	53962	49342	47581	47079	47249	47223	49325	51645	48565	50685	52739	51742	61022
21	45019	49654	50359	53257	49235	47579	47165	47212	47050	49004	51469	48310	50229	52610	57546
22	46048	44817	49335	50090	52530	49124	47577	47174	47171	46872	48673	51288	47849	50131	52476
23	44052	45754	44610	49008	49814	51784	49010	47576	47345	47135	46689	48333	50752	47728	50029
24	44278	43913	45454	44398	48674	49532	51021	48893	47574	47438	47096	46502	47923	50576	47603
25	44912	44012	43772	45146	44182	48331	49243	50241	48774	47572	47534	47055	46060	47656	50394
26	40440	44637	43741	43627	44833	43961	47983	48949	49446	48652	47570	47631	46584	45945	47787
27	40363	40184	44359	43466	43481	44515	43737	47629	48651	48639	48529	47568	47158	46446	45828
28	42435	40137	39926	44078	43189	43333	44195	43511	47273	48350	47826	48405	47119	47023	46307
29	40897	42154	39908	39666	43795	42909	43184	43872	43284	46913	48047	47005	47940	47007	46886
30	39448	40657	41868	39677	39402	43507	42626	43032	43544	43052	46548	47739	46553	47817	46892
31	37181	38975	40414	41579	39442	39135	43216	42338	42879	43212	42819	46178	47269	46434	47692
32	36887	36887	38495	40168	41286	39204	38864	42920	42047	42724	42875	42581	45767	47136	46313
33	37328	37553	36589	38008	39918	40988	38963	38589	42621	41751	42566	42533	42193	45683	47001
34	35729	37015	37174	36288	37516	39665	40688	38719	38311	42318	41453	42407	42043	42106	45598
35	36216	35320	36699	36792	35983	37019	39410	40384	38472	38030	42012	41151	42002	41852	42017
36	36202	35696	34907	36380	36407	35676	36518	39152	40078	38224	37747	41704	40689	41896	41656
37	35358	35713	35172	34491	36059	36019	35368	36013	38894	39770	37974	37462	41239	40519	41788
38	35012	34942	35223	34647	34075	35737	35630	35058	35508	38634	39461	37723	37049	41069	40345
39	34793	34546	34525	34731	34120	33656	35414	35240	34747	35000	38373	39151	37278	36901	40895
40	33476	34422	34073	34102	34232	33586	33232	35087	34844	34432	34486	38109	38677	37098	36749
41	29732	32873	34048	33597	33675	33730	33047	32805	34757	34445	34114	33967	37651	38477	36913
42	29789	29351	32273	33675	33123	33250	33229	32511	32379	34428	34048	33798	33568	37461	38274
43	30348	29364	28973	31678	33306	32653	32830	32733	31980	31958	34102	33655	33437	33409	37270
44	30877	30003	28938	28596	31084	32937	32184	32409	32238	31449	31537	33777	33236	33314	33247
45	29540	30486	29654	28507	28213	30482	32563	31708	31983	31736	30912	31110	33344	33050	33188
46	28572	29076	30085	29296	28066	27822	29865	32181	31221	31547	31222	30361	30682	33145	32858
47	29040	28139	28603	29676	28931	27616	27423	29236	31790	30724	31102	30697	29941	30469	32937
48	28495	28648	27695	28118	29257	28557	27155	27013	28592	31391	30215	30646	30282	29728	30246
49	27249	28035	28246	27240	27621	28828	28174	26682	26594	27932	30981	29694	30180	30077	29506

	1968	1969	1970	1971	1972	1973	1974	1975	1976	1977	1978	1979	1980	1981	1982
15	87613	91777	97288	88489	92821	95379	70057	69230	54513	78660	139047	125138	118625	124626	110395
16	85605	87483	91693	89895	92684	92684	95192	69947	69290	54423	78847	138700	124781	118878	124892
17	73125	85546	87341	91603	97002	88267	92534	94989	69827	69356	54325	78752	138322	124392	119158
18	73692	73001	85481	87184	91503	96837	88139	92369	94765	69695	69552	54217	79278	137904	123963
19	63538	73634	72867	85411	87015	91395	96659	88001	92190	94523	69552	69506	54101	79523	137453
20	61257	63491	73574	72727	75338	86838	91282	96473	87857	92004	94269	69402	69588	53979	79778
21	60913	61163	63442	73513	72583	85262	86657	91166	96282	87709	91812	94010	69249	69672	53854
22	57344	60800	61065	63392	73449	72434	85184	86468	91045	96084	87555	91614	93740	69089	69759
23	52337	57134	60683	60965	63340	73382	72280	85103	86273	90921	95879	87396	91408	93461	68925
24	49924	52194	56917	60562	60860	63287	73314	72121	85019	86072	90792	95667	87232	91196	93173
25	47474	49815	52047	56694	60437	60753	63232	73244	71956	84933	85864	90660	95449	87063	90977
26	50208	47342	49704	51895	56464	60309	60642	63175	73171	71787	84844	85651	90523	95225	86889
27	47717	50018	47207	49590	51740	56230	60178	60530	63117	73097	71615	84754	85433	90384	94996
28	45711	47646	49826	47070	49476	51584	55994	60047	60416	63058	73023	71441	84663	85213	90244
29	46165	45591	47573	49630	46932	49359	51425	55754	59912	60300	62999	72947	71264	84570	84990
30	46746	46020	45468	47500	49431	46790	49240	51262	55508	59775	60182	62938	72869	71083	84475
31	46775	46603	45871	45343	47424	49266	46644	49118	51096	55257	59635	60061	62876	72790	70898
32	47564	46655	46457	45720	45215	47347	49019	46497	48994	50927	55001	59492	59938	62613	72709
33	46189	47434	46534	46308	45566	45085	47269	48807	46346	48867	50755	54740	59346	59812	62748
34	46863	46063	47301	46409	46157	45408	44952	47189	48590	46192	48738	50578	54473	59198	59684
35	45511	46723	45934	47165	46283	46002	45248	44817	47107	48369	46036	48606	50399	54202	59046
36	41927	45422	46579	45802	47026	46153	45844	45084	44679	46944	48144	45875	48471	50215	53924
37	41458	41835	45332	46433	45668	46886	46022	45683	44918	44538	46939	47915	45713	48334	50029
38	41679	41257	41741	45240	46285	45532	46743	45886	45520	44395	44576	46853	47682	45547	48195
39	40168	41568	41051	41646	46147	46134	45394	46597	45752	45354	44576	44250	46765	47445	45379
40	40717	39986	41453	40840	41548	45050	45979	45252	46447	45612	45183	44399	44100	46675	47201
41	36593	40534	39799	41336	40624	41148	44952	45819	45106	46294	45468	45008	44217	43947	46583
42	36724	36431	40348	39609	41217	40405	41346	44852	45658	44958	46138	45323	44830	44033	43791
43	38069	36534	36273	40160	39418	41097	40182	41243	44751	45494	44808	45980	45175	44650	43846
44	37074	37859	36340	36110	39968	39222	40974	39956	41137	44647	45327	44655	45819	45025	44466
45	33080	36872	37642	36139	35940	39767	39020	40847	39721	41028	44540	45155	44497	45652	44869
46	33056	32905	36661	37417	35930	35764	39563	38809	40715	39477	40915	44429	44975	44332	45479
47	32657	32919	32724	36443	37192	35813	35581	39349	38590	40537	39233	40797	44314	44788	44161
48	32722	32449	32776	32536	36215	36939	35487	35390	39126	38363	40334	38959	40675	44194	44594
49	30014	32496	32231	32627	32339	36684	36684	35251	35191	38892	38125	40285	38684	40347	44068

Note: The number at a given age in a given year was determined by intra-cohort interpolation. For example, women at age 22-23 in 1958 were aged 17-18 in 1953 and aged 28-29 in 1964. The number is estimated as $_1N_{17}(53) - f(_1N_{17}(53) - _1N_{28}(64))$ when f is the expected fraction of the total cohort deaths from 1953 to 1964 that occurred while the cohort advanced from 1953 to 1958. This fraction was estimated as $(_1L_{17} - _1L_{22})/(_1L_{17} - _1L_{28})$ from a model life table (West level 9) which is about the proper level of mortality. West levels 15 interpolation factors were used for 1964-82. Note that the use of model life table interpolation factors does not ascribe the given level of mortality to the cohort to which the interpolation is applied. Only the distribution of deaths within each age interval is borrowed from the model table. The survival rate from one census date to the next is taken from the censuses themselves.

TABLE A-2 Population by Sex and Single Years of Age, 1953, 1964, and 1982 (after adjustment): China

Age	Female	Male	Sex Ratio	Age	Female	Male
1953[a]						
0	94001	98588		50	27996	29210
1	108081	114115		51	24582	26036
2	84684	90267		52	24923	25780
3	81241	88242		53	22365	22987
4	69997	76565		54	21082	22153
5	57637	74708		55	21710	23217
6	65575	73358		56	20458	21733
7	60068	67793		57	20193	20554
8	53831	61281		58	21083	20784
9	52301	50364		59	19655	19205
10	50492	58890		60	20899	20121
11	52925	61718		61	17311	16814
12	51531	60585		62	16402	15476
13	48291	57107		63	15876	14683
14	47443	56768		64	15690	14134
15	46697	55514		65	15170	13294
16	47587	55361	1.1634	66	13708	11975
17	49647	57168	1.1515	67	12748	10762
18	55327	63002	1.1387	68	12038	9790
19	50876	58537	1.1506	69	11009	8972
20	49963	57259	1.1460	70	11598	8977
21	45019	51387	1.1415	71	10078	7634
22	46048	52436	1.1387	72	9556	6882
23	44052	50042	1.1360	73	8209	5772
24	44278	50137	1.1323	74	6292	4298
25	44912	50732	1.1296	75	5736	3781
26	40440	45533	1.1259	76	5107	3231
27	40363	45336	1.1232	77	4397	2689
28	42435	47508	1.1195	78	4023	2340
29	40897	45674	1.1168	79	3300	1840
30	39448	43948	1.1141	80	2998	1577
31	37181	41321	1.1113	81	2162	1108
32	37927	42011	1.1077	82	1921	931
33	37328	41246	1.1050	83	1472	682
34	35729	39348	1.1013	84	1139	500
35	36216	39786	1.0986	85	910	387
36	36202	39671	1.0958	86	642	258
37	35358	38617	1.0922	87	461	177
38	35012	36143	1.0894	88	348	127
39	34793	38054		89	215	75
40	33476	36481		90	179	66
41	29732	33085		91	94	30
42	29789	32313		92	67	21
43	30348	32344		93	47	15
44	30877	32718		94	33	11
45	29540	31083		95	29	11
46	28572	30202		96	23	8
47	29040	29985		97	15	5
48	28495	29131		98	13	4
49	27249	28503		99	8	3
				100	17	16

[a]Adjustments for 1953: The male population aged 16-38 was inflated so as to match the estimated sequence of males/females by age, and to add in 6.8 million males (the difference between the population total for the official age distribution and the total listed as "well enumerated"). The whole population was inflated by 582.6/574.2 to allow for the 8.4 million "indirectly enumerated."

TABLE A-2 (continued)

Age	Female	Male	Sex Ratio	Age	Female	Male
1964[b]						
0	140747	145104		50	30559	31140
1	148386	155164		51	26553	26949
2	75983	80256		52	25259	25579
3	56138	59619		53	24641	24356
4	69044	74509		54	26069	24904
5	71768	77587		55	25947	24137
6	97666	107001		56	23658	21733
7	94414	103429		57	23014	20895
8	89702	97725		58	23957	21052
9	98615	107124		59	22462	19679
10	92773	100017		60	21973	19021
11	88714	95313		61	20792	17947
12	86440	92580		62	18900	15966
13	74092	80266		63	18500	15363
14	74416	81905		64	15975	12965
15	64154	70996		65	14236	11471
16	62033	69353	1.118	66	14278	11321
17	61764	69299	1.122	67	12912	10117
18	58531	65847	1.125	68	12486	9404
19	53245	60114	1.129	69	11815	8779
20	50685	57375	1.132	70	10768	7657
21	48310	54880	1.136	71	9917	6983
22	51288	58417	1.139	72	8835	5976
23	48333	55245	1.143	73	7569	4985
24	46502	53291	1.146	74	6982	4423
25	47055	54113	1.150	75	6325	3885
26	47631	54919	1.153	76	5555	3253
27	47568	53870		77	4715	2696
28	48405	54442		78	4061	2213
29	47005	52369		79	3309	1730
30	47739	53702		80	2813	1438
31	46178	51530		81	2358	1145
32	42581	47732		82	1934	891
33	42533	47562		83	1550	656
34	42407	46689		84	1186	488
35	41151	45145		85	738	303
36	41704	45607		86	544	212
37	37462	41539		87	414	151
38	37723	41154		88	306	107
39	39151	42480		89	210	73
40	38109	40734		90	151	55
41	33967	36327		91	86	29
42	33798	36130		92	60	21
43	33655	35709		93	42	16
44	33777	35494		94	33	14
45	31110	32329		95	28	14
46	30361	31550		96	22	10
47	30697	32036		97	15	7
48	30646	30949		98	14	7
49	29694	30254		99	11	7
				100	30	21

[b]Adjustments for 1964: The male population aged 16-26 was inflated so as to yield the indicated sequence of sex ratios, which added 2.35 million. The male population at every age was inflated by a factor of 1.0069 and the female by a factor of 1.0071 to allow for 4.9 million persons listed as age unknown.

TABLE A-2 (continued)

Age	Female	Male	Sex Ratio	Age	Female	Male
1982[c]						
0	100280	107820		50	40413	45293
1	83624	90173		51	38092	43421
2	88114	94629		52	39792	44674
3	94924	101313		53	37054	40770
4	90303	95988		54	37547	41452
5	94079	100134		55	33776	37048
6	98949	105211		56	33241	35930
7	105542	112211		57	34133	36435
8	116622	123685		58	33221	34765
9	121718	129165		59	29725	30820
10	122221	129948		60	30388	31222
11	132417	140861		61	28551	29081
12	128559	136396		62	28243	28578
13	137231	145161		63	25142	24594
14	118980	126250		64	24354	23672
15	110395	116975		65	24853	23282
16	124892	134796	1.079	66	23255	21589
17	119158	128607	1.079	67	21606	19912
18	123963	133793	1.079	68	22265	20187
19	137453	148353	1.079	69	18943	16781
20	79778	86104	1.079	70	17427	15101
21	53854	58125	1.079	71	16627	14061
22	69759	75291	1.079	72	16054	13038
23	68925	73977		73	15543	12006
24	93173	101287		74	13449	10184
25	90977	97922		75	12204	8892
26	86889	92329		76	11732	8166
27	94996	101737		77	10935	6873
28	90244	95934		78	9096	5985
29	84990	89893		79	8043	5060
30	84475	89089		80	6944	4235
31	70898	75406		81	5792	3384
32	72709	80061		82	4466	2503
33	62748	68850		83	3407	1843
34	59684	65659		84	2960	1532
35	59046	65083		85	2341	1188
36	53924	59015		86	1839	853
37	50029	55607		87	1440	638
38	48195	54214		88	1054	453
39	45379	51542		89	774	307
40	47201	53288		90	618	248
41	46583	53332		91	384	137
42	43791	49871		92	277	99
43	43846	50021		93	184	60
44	44466	51412		94	117	44
45	44869	51047		95	98	37
46	45379	51050		96	57	23
47	44161	48790		97	40	18
48	44594	49955		98	31	15
49	44068	49628		99	22	11
				100	27	11

[c]Adjustments for 1982: The number of female members of the armed forces were allocated as follows: 20 percent to age 19; 60 percent to age 20; and 20 percent to age 21. The number of males at each age from 16-22 was estimated as 1.079 times the number of females at the same age, adding 4.1 million males and 0.1 million females, totaling the listed 4.2 million military personnel.

TABLE A-3 Proportion of Children Born Alive Who Were Born in Specified Years, by Age of Mother, 1982: China

Year of Birth	Age of Mother							
	15-19	20-24	25-29	30-34	35-39	40-44	45-49	50-54
81-82	.681	.398	.144	.030	.009	.003	.001	.000
80-81	.219	.254	.146	.036	.010	.004	.001	.000
79-80	.066	.152	.141	.050	.014	.005	.001	.000
78-79	.027	.093	.132	.066	.020	.008	.002	.000
77-78	.007	.052	.109	.074	.025	.010	.004	.001
76-77		.028	.093	.083	.032	.015	.006	.001
75-76		.014	.077	.090	.042	.020	.009	.002
74-75		.005	.062	.095	.053	.026	.013	.004
73-74		.002	.044	.096	.064	.035	.018	.006
72-73		.001	.027	.090	.072	.043	.024	.010
71-72			.016	.083	.079	.050	.031	.014
70-71			.007	.073	.084	.058	.036	.019
69-70			.003	.055	.085	.061	.040	.024
68-69			.001	.039	.086	.068	.045	.029
67-68				.022	.077	.068	.046	.031
66-67				.012	.067	.067	.047	.034
65-66				.006	.060	.071	.052	.040
64-65				.002	.049	.070	.054	.041
63-64				.001	.039	.075	.061	.049
62-63					.023	.072	.065	.052
61-62					.008	.046	.047	.037
60-61					.003	.030	.037	.030
59-60					.001	.026	.040	.035
58-59					.001	.025	.046	.043
57-58						.022	.054	.051
56-57						.013	.052	.053
55-56						.007	.046	.052
54-55						.003	.041	.054
53-54						.001	.032	.052
52-53							.023	.052
51-52							.014	.047
50-51							.007	.041
Before 1950							.004	.063

TABLE A-4 Proportion of Ever-Married Women (per 1,000 women) by Single Years of Age, Aged 15-35, Constructed from First Marriage Rates, 1950-81, and Reported in the Sample Survey, 1981: China

	1950	1951	1952	1953	1954	1955	1956	1957	1958	1959	1960	1961	1962	1963	1964	1965	1966
15	65	74	54	40	35	32	31	29	28	25	23	23	24	24	19	14	12
16	219	211	192	158	137	125	118	113	107	98	90	89	95	92	79	64	50
17	412	375	360	337	307	281	261	253	246	225	206	205	215	222	195	160	136
18	574	565	533	518	495	475	451	426	418	394	362	358	377	392	369	314	270
19	694	704	693	672	652	636	629	604	573	552	528	512	538	561	543	497	434
20	795	799	803	794	777	756	746	747	718	675	661	658	666	694	687	647	603
21	861	867	869	870	861	849	830	823	825	790	754	760	775	783	790	763	724
22	905	907	911	915	912	906	897	878	872	873	843	821	844	858	849	848	819
23	931	934	937	942	944	940	936	931	913	905	909	890	880	901	903	890	890
24	950	952	954	956	961	963	960	958	952	934	929	941	929	919	935	931	918
25	967	967	968	969	971	975	976	974	971	965	949	949	965	954	941	954	952
26	977	978	977	977	978	980	984	985	982	980	975	961	964	979	966	954	970
27	983	984	984	983	983	985	987	990	990	988	986	982	970	972	987	974	963
28	987	986	986	988	987	988	989	991	993	993	991	991	988	975	977	991	978
29	991	990	990	991	992	990	991	992	993	995	995	994	994	991	978	979	993
30	993	993	992	992	994	993	992	993	993	995	996	996	995	996	993	981	981
31	994	994	994	994	994	995	995	994	994	994	996	998	998	997	997	994	982
32	995	995	995	995	995	995	996	995	995	995	995	997	998	998	997	997	995
33	997	996	996	997	996	996	996	997	996	995	996	996	998	999	998	998	998
34	997	998	997	997	997	997	997	997	997	996	996	997	997	998	999	999	998
35	997	998	998	998	998	998	998	997	997	997	997	997	997	998	998	999	999

	1967	1968	1969	1970	1971	1972	1973	1974	1975	1976	1977	1978	1979	1980	1981	1982
15	10	10	9	8	8	6	5	5	5	4	3	3	2	2	2	2
16	42	42	41	36	31	26	20	17	17	14	12	11	9	9	10	8
17	116	109	110	100	84	71	58	45	39	36	30	28	26	24	26	24
18	249	231	225	218	188	157	134	109	89	76	69	61	59	61	60	60
19	401	390	374	361	337	292	245	207	173	144	127	117	108	115	128	121
20	553	538	540	513	480	445	389	332	286	246	213	194	184	186	226	261
21	696	670	674	669	617	572	537	480	421	375	333	301	290	295	329	384
22	790	785	776	775	755	696	651	622	570	518	478	441	419	427	463	508
23	869	855	862	849	840	818	759	723	705	668	625	593	572	569	612	668
24	924	914	909	915	895	884	866	814	790	789	762	727	716	719	739	793
25	942	955	951	943	946	924	917	906	861	848	860	841	821	835	852	879
26	969	961	977	971	960	962	944	942	936	899	895	913	903	899	921	927
27	981	981	973	987	979	969	974	958	960	960	926	925	949	947	945	960
28	969	988	988	979	992	984	976	981	966	973	975	942	944	971	969	979
29	981	973	993	992	981	995	988	980	985	972	979	984	954	956	982	985
30	995	983	975	995	993	983	997	990	982	988	974	984	990	961	962	988
31	982	996	985	976	995	995	985	998	992	984	990	977	987	994	965	991
32	983	983	997	985	976	996	996	986	999	993	986	991	978	989	996	990
33	996	983	984	997	985	977	996	996	986	999	993	986	992	979	990	995
34	999	996	983	984	997	985	977	997	997	986	999	993	987	993	980	995
35	999	999	996	983	984	997	986	977	997	997	987	1000	994	988	994	996

Note: The first marriage rate given for the earliest age (15) in a given year is approximately equal to the proportion ever married at exact age 16 at the end of the year. Addition of the first-marriage rate at 16 in the next year yields the proportion ever married at exact age 17 at the end of that year. For a given year (say 1970) and a given single-year age interval (say, 20 to 21), there are four relevant calculable proportions of ever-married women: at exact ages 20 and 21 at the beginning and end of the year. The proportion ever married at 20 to 21 in mid-1970 is taken as the arithmetic mean of these four numbers.

TABLE A-5 Number of Ever-Married Women (in 100s) by Duration Since First Marriage, 1970-82: China

	1970	1971	1972	1973	1974	1975	1976	1977	1978	1979	1980	1981	1982
0	63774	57380	54166	53399	53596	56004	60271	63828	67433	74804	87422	101710	115044
1	64462	63653	57273	54065	53292	53487	55883	60136	63679	67163	74659	87257	101529
2	56053	64329	63531	57159	53955	53182	53371	55760	59996	63425	67036	74512	87088
3	46590	55929	64193	63400	57042	53845	53068	53249	55633	59759	63301	66903	74362
4	41157	46476	55801	64052	63268	56925	53732	52949	53128	55415	59639	63173	66766
5	41271	41047	46365	55671	63911	63131	56804	53613	52827	52920	55308	59524	63044
6	47509	41152	40937	46247	55541	63764	62995	56680	53493	52623	52819	55199	59402
7	55878	47357	41030	40823	46126	55405	63615	62852	56548	53288	52523	52715	55086
8	54014	55698	47205	40903	40708	46006	55268	63462	62706	56333	53187	52422	52610
9	45300	53836	55514	47052	40775	40587	45883	55126	63305	62461	56227	53087	52318
10	38747	45186	53624	55326	46895	40646	40470	45794	54982	63014	62343	56121	52983
11	38230	38623	45035	53409	55135	46736	40514	40389	45665	54718	62884	62220	56010
12	41338	38109	38494	44854	53222	54941	46607	40383	40261	45432	54595	62752	62093
13	42024	41237	37981	38336	44699	53031	54744	46443	40242	40038	45316	54469	62613
14	41703	41920	41099	37863	38207	44538	52839	54510	46271	40007	39924	45204	54341
15	40837	41568	41778	40970	37773	38069	44342	52649	54264	45991	39882	39852	45048
16	40353	40703	41427	41614	40867	37673	37895	44189	52368	53936	45875	39757	39743
17	40503	40218	40560	41261	41507	40718	37537	37772	43942	52055	53748	45759	39634
18	40846	40371	40078	40403	41117	41389	40570	37418	37550	43635	51868	53594	45605
19	42855	40745	40229	39894	40300	40996	41202	40445	37197	37320	43478	51731	53371
20+	426534	434765	440660	446463	448001	449403	453142	456971	456900	453781	449152	452197	461760

Note: Calculated from first marriage frequencies at each age for each cohort, the proportion ever married (Table A-4) and the number of women (Table A-1).

TABLE A-6 Number of Births and Marital Fertility Rate at
Each Duration of Marriage, 1970, 1977, and 1981: China

	Number of Births			Duration-Specific Fertility		
	1970	1977	1981	1970	1977	1981
0	513	833	1730	.08087	.13084	.17009
1	3152	3243	5705	.49156	.54068	.65382
2	2265	1892	2562	.40623	.34018	.34384
3	1826	1723	2051	.39401	.32440	.30656
4	1545	1525	1597	.37735	.28875	.25280
5	1302	1450	1302	.31711	.27113	.21874
6	1372	1252	1046	.29030	.22144	.18950
7	1600	1234	809	.28783	.19682	.15347
8	1741	1082	729	.32401	.17091	.13906
9	1326	904	609	.29424	.16438	.11472
10	1198	687	488	.31080	.15038	.08695
11	914	542	479	.24030	.13452	.07698
12	1087	461	376	.26432	.11443	.05992
13	976	414	311	.23344	.08936	.05710
14	1024	391	270	.24680	.07190	.05973
15	900	403	187	.22152	.07672	.04692
16	873	313	170	.21747	.07100	.04276
17	793	314	148	.19679	.08333	.03234
18	767	217	138	.18874	.05813	.02575
19	685	218	142	.16067	.05403	.02745
20+	3436	899	493	.08099	.01972	.01090

REFERENCES AND BIBLIOGRAPHY

Barclay, G. W., A. J. Coale, M. A. Stoto, and T. J. Trussell (1976) A reassessment of the demography of traditional rural China. Population Index 42(4).
Brass, W., A. J. Coale, P. Demeny, D. F. Heisel, F. Lorimer, A. Romaniuk, and E. van de Walle (1968) The Demography of Tropical Africa. Princeton, N.J.: Princeton University Press.
China, Population Census Office Under the State Council and State Statistical Bureau (1983) Major Figures by 10 Percent Sampling Tabulation on the 1982 Population Census of the People's Republic of China. Beijing: State Statistical Bureau.
Coale, A. J. (1971) Age patterns of marriage. Population Studies 25(2).
Coale, A. J. (1984) Construction of a life table from accurate enumeration of a closed population in two censuses. Population Index (forthcoming).
Coale, A. J., and D. R. McNeil (1972) The distribution by age of the frequency of first marriage in a female cohort. Journal of the American Statistical Association 67(340).
Coale, A. J., and T. J. Trussell (1974) Model fertility schedules: variations in the age structure of childbearing in human populations. Population Index 40(2):185-258.
Henry, L. (1961) Some data on national fertility. Eugenics Quarterly 8:81:91.
Hook, B., ed. (1982) The Cambridge Encyclopedia of China. New York: Cambridge University Press.
Jiang, Z. H., W. M. Zhang, and L. W. Zhu (1984) The Preliminary Study of the Life Expectancy at Birth for China's Population. International Seminar on China's 1982 Population Census, Beijing.

Kaplan, F. M., J. Sobin, and S. Andors (1980) *Encyclopedia of China Today*. New York: Harper & Row.

Li, C. (1983a) On the results of the Chinese census. *Population and Development Review* 9(2):325-344.

Li, C. (1983b) The Quality Control of the 1982 Population Census of China. Paper presented at the meeting of the International Statistical Institute, Madrid.

Li, H., T. Song, and C. Li (1983) Current fertility state of women of Han and minority nationalities in rural areas. *Population and Economics* Special Issue: 92-97.

Li, M. (1982) The focal point of China's population is in the rural areas. *Population and Economics* (Nov.).

Li, X., and Z. Zhang (1983) Occupation and fertility level of women of reproductive age. *Population and Economics* Special Issue: 83-85.

Liao, T., and Y. Wen (1982) *The Theory of Two Kinds of Production and China's Population Problem*. Canton: Quandong People's Press.

Liu, C., and Z. Li (1983) Sex composition of population. *Population and Economics* Special Issue: 145.

Population Reference Bureau (1983) *World Population Data Sheet*. New York: Population Reference Bureau.

Preston, S. H., and A. J. Coale (1982) Age structure, growth, attrition, and accession: a new synthesis. *Population Index* 48:217-259.

Qiu, S., S. Wu, and M. Wang (1983) Birth control of women of reproductive age. *Population and Economics* Special Issue: 130-136.

Ryder, N. B. (1956) Problems of trend determination during a transition in fertility. *Milbank Memorial Fund Quarterly* 34(1).

Song, Y., Y. Shi, and G. Zhang (1983) The order-birth of women's fertility. *Population and Economics* Special Issue: 56-61.

State Statistical Bureau (1982) *The 1982 Population Census of China*. Population Census Office, State Council, and Department of Population Statistics. Beijing: State Statistical Office.

State Statistical Bureau (1983a) *Statistical Yearbook of China, 1983* (English edition). Economic Information Agency. Hong Kong: State Statistical Bureau.

State Statistical Bureau (1983b) *Major Figures by 10 Percent Sampling Tabulation on the 1982 Popuation Census of the People's Republic of China*. Population

Census Office, State Council, and Department of Population Statistics. Beijing: State Statistical Bureau.

Tien, H. Y. (1983) Age at marriage in the People's Republic of China. <u>The China Quarterly</u> (93).

United Nations (1983) <u>Indirect Techniques for Demographic Estimation</u>, Manual X. New York: United Nations.

Xiao, Z. (1983) The design of the sample survey. <u>Population and Economics</u> Special Issue: 10-22.

Yu, W., and Z. Xiao (1983) The general introduction of the national one-per-thousand-population sample survey in birth rate and an initial analysis of data concerned. <u>Population and Economics</u> Special Issue: 3-9.

Zhao, J., and J. Sun (1983) Educational and fertility level of women of reproductive age. <u>Population and Economics</u> Special Issue: 80-82.

Zhao, W., and H. Yu (1983) Changes of women's age at first marriage since liberation. <u>Population and Economics</u> Special Issue: 115-118.